Student Applications Book

Great Source Education Group
a Houghton Mifflin Company
Wilmington, Massachusetts

www.greatsource.com

AUTHORS

Laura Robb
Author

Powhatan School, Boyce, Virginia
Laura Robb, author of *Reading Strategies That Work* and *Teaching Reading in Middle School,* has taught language arts at Powhatan School in Boyce, Virginia, for more than 30 years. She is a co-author of the *Reading and Writing Sourcebooks* for grades 3–5 and the *Summer Success: Reading* program. Robb also mentors and coaches teachers in Virginia public schools and speaks at conferences throughout the country on reading and writing.

Ron Klemp
Contributing Author

Los Angeles Unified School District, Los Angeles, California
Ron Klemp is the Coordinator of Reading for the Los Angeles Unified School District. He has taught Reading, English, and Social Studies and was a middle school Dean of Discipline. He is also coordinator/facilitator at the Secondary Practitioner Center, a professional development program in the Los Angeles Unified School District. He has been teaching at California State University, Cal Lutheran University, and National University.

Wendell Schwartz
Contributing Author

Adlai Stevenson High School, Lincolnshire, Illinois
Wendell Schwartz has been a teacher of English for 36 years. For the last 24 years he also has served as the Director of Communication Arts at Adlai Stevenson High School. He has taught gifted middle school students for the last 12 years, as well as teaching graduate-level courses for National-Louis University in Evanston, Illinois.

Editorial: Developed by Nieman, Inc.
Design: Ronan Design: Christine Ronan, Sean O'Neill, Maria Mariottini
Illustrations: Mike McConnell

Trademarks and trade names are shown in this book strictly for illustrative purposes and are the property of their respective owners. The author's references herein should not be regarded as affecting their validity.

Copyright © 2002 by Great Source Education Group, Inc. All rights reserved. Great Source® is a registered trademark of Houghton Mifflin Company.

Permission is hereby granted to teachers who have purchased the *Reader's Handbook* and the Complete Program Package (Grade 6, ISBN 0-669-49093-8) to reprint or photocopy in classroom quantities the pages or sheets in this work that carry a copyright notice, provided each copy made shows the copyright notice. Such copies may not be sold and further distribution is expressly prohibited. Except as authorized above, prior written permission must be obtained from Great Source Education Group, Inc., to reproduce or transmit this work or portions thereof in any other form or by any other electronic or mechanical means, including any information storage or retrieval system, unless expressly permitted by federal copyright law. Address inquiries to Great Source Education Group, Inc., 181 Ballardvale Street, Wilmington, Massachusetts 01887.

Printed in the United States of America

International Standard Book Number: 0-669-49096-2
(Student Applications Book)

1 2 3 4 5 6 7 8 9—DBH—08 07 06 05 04 03 02

International Standard Book Number: 0-669-49081-4
(Student Applications Book, Teacher's Edition)

1 2 3 4 5 6 7 8 9—DBH—08 07 06 05 04 03 02

Table of Contents for Student Applications Book

Lesson

© GREAT SOURCE. ALL RIGHTS RESERVED.

© GREAT SOURCE. ALL RIGHTS RESERVED.

© GREAT SOURCE. ALL RIGHTS RESERVED.

What Happens When You Read

What happens when you read? What do you see in your mind as "reading"? You probably ask yourself a series of questions each time you pick up a book.

Visualizing Reading

Reading is a process. It occurs over time—a few minutes, a few hours, or even a few days if the book is very, very long or very, very good.

Directions: Draw a picture of yourself reading a really great book. Use "balloons" to show what you are thinking.

© GREAT SOURCE. ALL RIGHTS RESERVED.

NAME FOR USE WITH PAGES 26–29

Questions for Readers

Asking yourself questions about what you are reading should be automatic. The questions you ask yourself have to do with why you're reading the book, what you expect to get out of it, and how long it's going to take.

Directions: Pick out a book from the classroom library that you might like to read sometime. Write the title on the line below. Then ask and answer some questions about it.

Title:

What are you reading about?

Why are you reading?

What do you want to get out of your reading?

What kind of reading is it?

Should you read slowly or quickly?

What can you do if you don't understand something?

How can you remember what you've read?

How do you know if you've understood it?

Should you read it more than once?

© GREAT SOURCE. ALL RIGHTS RESERVED.

The Reading Process

The reading process is what you do to get more *from a text.*

Your Reading Process

Everyone has habits when it comes to reading. What are yours? What do you do before, during, and after reading?

Directions: Describe your own reading process. Make notes or write in full sentences.

Before Reading

During Reading

After Reading

© GREAT SOURCE. ALL RIGHTS RESERVED.

NAME ____________ FOR USE WITH PAGES 32-37

The Handbook's Reading Process

Think of the reading process as a road map that can lead you through the different kinds of reading. This road map can prevent you from getting lost. The handbook you have in front of you has lots of suggestions about the reading process.

Directions: Skim pages 32–36. Then use your own words to tell about the steps in the reading process described in the handbook.

Before Reading

....

....

....

....

During Reading

....

....

....

After Reading

....

....

....

....

If you get stuck, look at the Summing Up section on page 37.

© GREAT SOURCE. ALL RIGHTS RESERVED.

Reading Know-how

You already have all kinds of reading know-how. All you need to do is figure out how to put it to use. Begin by sharpening your most important thinking skills.

Thinking Skill 1: Making Inferences

Writers don't tell you everything. Sometimes you need to figure things out on your own. This means that you need to make inferences, or reasonable guesses, about what is going on in a text.

Directions: Read the paragraph in the box. Then make inferences. Circle the answer that completes each sentence and write how you know the answer.

A group of twenty young people, all about twelve years old, board a bus that says "D.C. Tours." The young people have suitcases and lunchboxes. They also carry notebooks and pencils. A man and woman are with the group. They wear shirts that say New York Public Schools. They both have clipboards and pencils.

My Inferences

The twenty young people are all _____. students camp counselors cousins

How I know this:

The group is on its way to _____. school Washington, D.C. a football game

How I know this:

The two adults are ______. tour guides teachers youth ministers

How I know this:

© GREAT SOURCE. ALL RIGHTS RESERVED.

NAME .... FOR USE WITH PAGES 40–42

Thinking Skill 2: Drawing Conclusions

Drawing conclusions means putting together bits of information and figuring out what they mean. It is putting two and two together to get four.

Directions: Think again about the people boarding the bus. Read the facts on the left. Write your conclusions on the right.

Facts		What I Concluded
Fact 1.	There are twenty young people in a group.	
Fact 2.	People board a bus that says "D.C. Tours."	
Fact 3.	The kids carry suitcases and lunches.	
Fact 4.	Two adults wear shirts that say New York Public Schools.	
Fact 5.	The adults have clipboards and pencils.	

© GREAT SOURCE. ALL RIGHTS RESERVED.

Thinking Skill 3: Comparing and Contrasting

Comparing and contrasting means noticing how things are alike and different.

Directions: Put two books on your desk. Compare them. Look at size, shape, thickness, and appearance. Write your notes on this Venn Diagram.

Venn Diagram

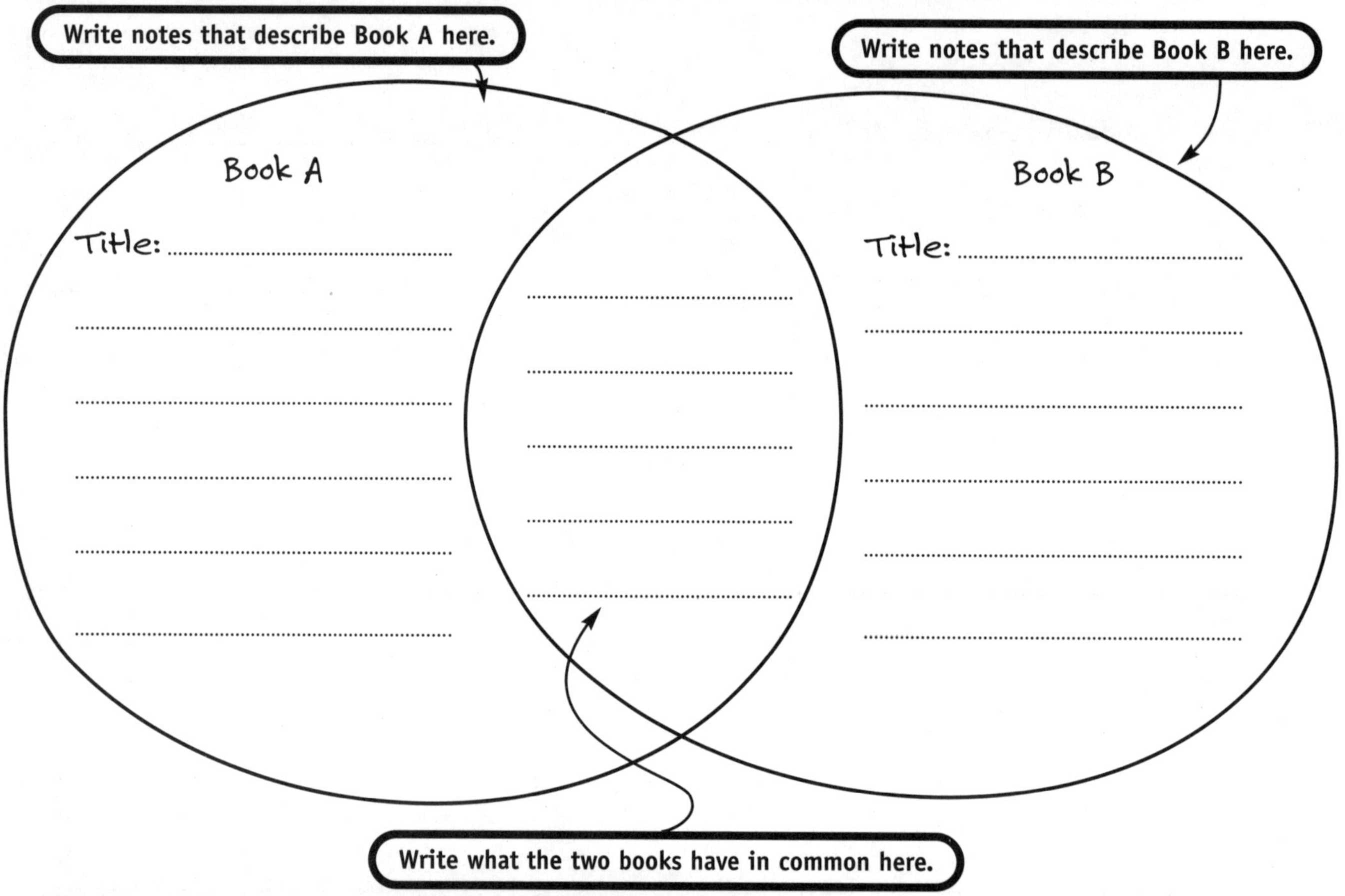
Write notes that describe Book A here.
Write notes that describe Book B here.
Book A
Title:
Book B
Title:
Write what the two books have in common here.

Thinking Skill 4: Evaluating

When you evaluate, you make a judgment. You say what you do and don't like about something. Then you explain your reasons.

Directions: Examine the two books again. Then tell which book looks more interesting. Explain why.

I think .... looks more interesting

because ....

....

© GREAT SOURCE. ALL RIGHTS RESERVED.

NAME FOR USE WITH PAGES 43–46

Reading Actively

Reading actively means making an effort to understand what you are reading. Active readers ask themselves questions, make predictions, and look for ways to connect to what they are reading. They make inferences, draw conclusions, compare, contrast, and evaluate.

Ways of Reading Actively

Good readers mark or highlight a text as they read. They react and connect, ask questions, visualize, predict, and make comments that clarify what the author is saying.

Directions: Turn to page 45 of the handbook. Read the section called "Ways of Reading Actively." Then do an active reading of this short passage from the novel *Treasure Island.*

from *Treasure Island* by Robert Louis Stevenson

1. Mark

Highlight information about time and place here.

SQUIRE TRELAWNEY, Dr. Livesey, and the rest of these gentlemen having asked me to write down the whole particulars about Treasure Island, from the beginning to the end, keeping nothing back but the bearings of the island, and that only because there is still treasure not yet lifted, I take up my pen in the year of grace 17__ and go back to the time when my father kept the Admiral Benbow inn and the brown old seaman with the saber cut first took up his lodging under our roof.

2. Question

Ask a question about the old brown seaman here.

....

....

....

....

© GREAT SOURCE. ALL RIGHTS RESERVED.

from *Treasure Island* by Robert Louis Stevenson, continued

I remember him as if it were yesterday, as he came plodding to the inn door, his sea-chest following behind him in a handbarrow—a tall, strong, heavy, nut-brown man, his tarry pigtail falling over the shoulder of his soiled blue coat, his hands ragged and scarred, with black, broken nails, and the saber cut across one cheek, a dirty, livid white. I remember him looking round the cover and whistling to himself as he did so, and then breaking out in that old sea song that he sang so often afterwards:

"Fifteen men on the dead man's chest—

Yo-ho-ho, and a bottle of rum!"

in the high, old tottering voice that seemed to have been tuned and broken at the capstan bars. Then he rapped on the door with a bit of stick like a handspike that he carried, . . . still looking about him at the cliffs and up at our signboard.

3. React

Tell where you've heard this tune before.

4. Predict

Predict what the seaman will say first.

5. Clarify

Write notes to pull together what you have learned about the narrator here.

6. Visualize

Make a sketch of the Admiral Benbow inn here.

© GREAT SOURCE. ALL RIGHTS RESERVED.

NAME .... FOR USE WITH PAGES 47–63

Reading Paragraphs

Each sentence in a paragraph contains a single thought, and each paragraph in a text explores a single large idea. Follow these steps to analyze a paragraph.

Step 1: Read the paragraph.

Begin by doing an active reading of the paragraph.

Directions: Read this paragraph from Abraham Lincoln's famous speech, "A House Divided." Make notes on the "stickies."

from "A House Divided" by Abraham Lincoln, 1858

We are now far into the fifth year since a policy was initiated with the avowed object and confident promise of putting an end to slavery agitation. Under the operation of that policy, that agitation has not only not ceased, but has constantly augmented. In my opinion, it will not cease until a crisis shall have been reached and passed. A house divided against itself cannot stand. I believe this Government cannot endure permanently half slave and half free. I do not expect the Union to be dissolved; I do not expect the house to fall; but I do expect it will cease to be divided. It will become all one thing or all the other. Either the opponents of slavery will arrest the further spread of it, and place it where the public mind shall rest in the belief that it is in the course of ultimate extinction, or its advocates will push it forward, till it shall become alike lawful in all the States, old as well as new, North as well as South.

Highlight/Mark

I found these repeated words:

....

....

....

Question

Ask yourself a question about the main idea in this paragraph.

My question: ....

....

....

....

Clarify

I think Lincoln meant this by "A house divided against itself cannot stand":

....

....

....

© GREAT SOURCE. ALL RIGHTS RESERVED.

Step 2: Find the subject.

To find the subject, ask yourself, "What is this paragraph mostly about?" You can find the subject by looking at these things:

- **the title**
- **the first sentence**
- **key or repeated words or names**

Directions: Answer these questions. They can help you explore the subject of the paragraph from Lincoln's speech.

What does the title of the speech mean?

What is the first sentence about?

What repeated words did you notice?

What do you think is the subject of the paragraph?

© GREAT SOURCE. ALL RIGHTS RESERVED.

NAME .... FOR USE WITH PAGES 47–63

Step 3: Find the main idea.

Stated Main Idea
Some writers state the main idea directly. The paragraph has what is called a "stated main idea." Often the stated main idea will be the first sentence or last sentence of a paragraph. Other times, as in this paragraph from Lincoln's speech, the main idea sentence appears somewhere in the middle.

Directions: Reread the paragraph from Lincoln's speech. Circle the main idea sentence. Then write the sentence here.

Lincoln's stated main idea: ....

....

....

....

I know this because ....

....

....

....

Implied Main Idea
Often the main idea of a paragraph is implied. This means it's not directly stated. When this is the case, you need to make inferences about the main idea. You do this by asking yourself, "What is the writer trying to tell me about the subject?"

Directions: Write what you think Lincoln is trying to tell his audience about the subject of slavery.

I think Lincoln is trying to say that ....

....

....

....

....

© GREAT SOURCE. ALL RIGHTS RESERVED.

Step 4: Find details that support the main idea.

Good writers support their main ideas with facts and details. A Main Idea Organizer can help you see how the main idea and details work together.

Directions: Complete this organizer. Use the notes you made about Lincoln's speech.

Main Idea Organizer

Write what you think is the biggest, most important idea here.

Title: "A House Divided"

Main Idea

Detail #1	**Detail #2**	**Detail #3**

Then write details here.

© GREAT SOURCE. ALL RIGHTS RESERVED.

NAME FOR USE WITH PAGES 66–83

Reading History

Reading history means paying attention to names, dates, and important details. It also means thinking about events that have made the world what it is today.

Textbooks

Before Reading

A history textbook is based on fact. It provides information and insight about events in history. Your job as a critical reader is to find the facts and decide what they mean. Use the reading process and the strategy of note-taking to help you read and understand the textbook chapter "Understanding Sumer."

A Set a Purpose

When reading history, your purpose is to find answers to these five questions: *who, what, where, when,* and *why*.

- **Use the 5 W's as your purpose for reading.**

Directions: Ask five questions about "Understanding Sumer." You will answer your questions later.

1.

2.

3.

4.

5.

© GREAT SOURCE. ALL RIGHTS RESERVED.

B Preview the Reading

Preview before you begin reading. Pay special attention to the first and last paragraphs, the headings, and any photos, diagrams, or maps.

Directions: Run your eyes over the chapter "Understanding Sumer." Then return to your five purpose questions and answer as many as you can.

© GREAT SOURCE. ALL RIGHTS RESERVED.

NAME FOR USE WITH PAGES 66–83

Textbooks

Chapter 2 Understanding Sumer

Study Guide

Main Idea: An area of Mesopotamia known as Sumer is considered the birthplace of civilization.

Goals: As you read, look for answers to these questions:

1. Where was Sumer located?
2. What problems did the earliest Sumerians face?
3. What was Uruk?
4. What important contributions did the Sumerians make to society?

Dates to Know

c. 5000 BC Ubaidian culture established in Sumer.

c. 4000 BC Uruk becomes Sumerian center of power. Sumerians invent wheel, ox-drawn plough, and writing.

Key Terms

nomads
polytheism
city-states
deity
surplus

Mesopotamia grew up between two great rivers of the Middle East: the Euphrates and the Tigris. Mesopotamia, whose name means "between two rivers," included all of present-day Iraq and parts of Syria and Turkey. On the southern half of Mesopotamia lay a region known as Sumer **(see Figure 2.1).** Sumer is often called the birthplace of civilization.

Figure 2.1 Ancient Mesopotamia, 5300-2350 BC

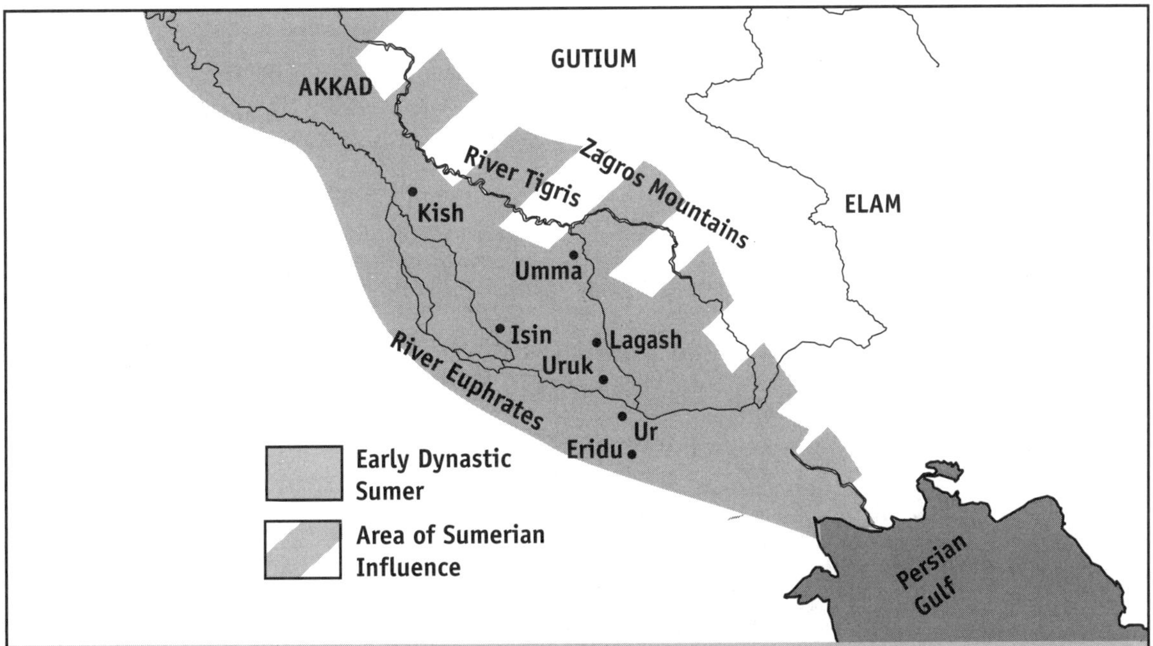

Map Search

Use the map to locate the southern half of Mesopotamia, a region known as Sumer.

© GREAT SOURCE. ALL RIGHTS RESERVED.

Early Sumerians

The earliest Sumerian culture is known as Ubaid. The Ubaidians settled in Sumer sometime around 5000 BC. These early Sumerians were mostly **nomads,** or people who followed their flocks and herds. The nomads came down from the Mesopotamian mountains with the hope that they could farm the land alongside the Euphrates. They were the first Sumerians.

For years, the early Sumerians tried in vain to raise crops. Although the banks alongside the Euphrates River were flat and fertile, there was little rain. Each spring, however, the Euphrates would flood and drown the crops the farmers had planted. Eventually, the Sumerians learned how to build irrigation canals to store the water and protect their farmland from flooding. These irrigation canals were the first major achievements of the Sumerians.

Eventually, more and more nomads came down from the mountains and settled in Sumer. They too had the dream of farming on the banks of the Euphrates and were amazed by the complex irrigation canals that had been built by Sumerians of long ago. Over the course of a thousand years, three of the larger Sumerian settlements, Eridu, Ur, and Uruk, grew into cities and eventually **city-states.** A city-state was a self-governing unit made up of a city and its surrounding villages and farmland.

By 4000 BC, the city-state of Uruk was the Sumerian center of power. In Uruk, there was a **surplus,** or excess, of food, thanks to the sophisticated farming methods the Urukians were using. As a result, people felt free to work at other occupations. Many became craftspeople and traders. Others practiced the art of writing, which was invented in Sumer around 3000 BC. Eventually, some Sumerians became priests who began teaching people about religion.

A limestone tablet with a Sumerian pictograph from 4000 BC

© GREAT SOURCE. ALL RIGHTS RESERVED.

NAME

The Sumerian Religion

The Sumerians practiced **polytheism,** the worship of many gods. Sumerians believed that there were hundreds of gods and goddesses who were responsible for controlling all living things **(see Figure 2.2)**. Each Sumerian city-state had its own patron **deity,** or god, to look over the welfare of the city. To show their respect for the patron deity, Sumerians built huge jeweled temples in the center of the city. Each day, people would gather at the temple to pay their respects and make offerings to the god.

Sumerian Priests and Kings

The earliest Sumerian cities were ruled by priests, not kings. By 3000 BC, however, Sumerian priests realized they needed military protection against invading nomads, who were jealous of the wealth they saw in the city-state of Sumer.

To protect themselves against attack, Sumerian priests began choosing strong military leaders from among the Sumerian citizens. Eventually the military leaders became full-time rulers. These new kings shared power with the Sumerian priests and were chiefly responsible for managing irrigation and farming. Eventually, the kings also became the chief judges of the land.

Name	Characteristics
Enki	Ruler of water, crafts, learning, and magic
Ninhursag	Great mother goddess, wife of Enlil, god of the air
Nanna	Moon god, son of Enlil
Utu	Son of Nanna, god of the sun
Inanna	Goddess of love and war, later renamed Ishtar

Figure 2.2 Important Sumerian Gods

C Plan

Your preview probably provided you with some quick answers to your 5 W's questions. During your careful reading, you'll want to make additional notes about facts and details that relate to the 5 W's.

- **Use the strategy of note-taking to keep track of what you learn.**

© GREAT SOURCE. ALL RIGHTS RESERVED.

During Reading

Now go back and read "Understanding Sumer." Read slowly and carefully.

D Read with a Purpose

Be sure to keep in mind your reading purpose of finding answers to *who, what, where, when,* and *why*.

Directions: Make some notes on the 5 W's Organizer below as you read. Be as detailed as possible.

5 W's Organizer

Subject

Who	What	Where	When	Why
the Sumerians				

© GREAT SOURCE. ALL RIGHTS RESERVED.

NAME FOR USE WITH PAGES 66–83

Using the Strategy

A 5 W's Organizer is just one way of organizing your reading notes. There are actually many different note-taking options.

- **Paragraph-by-Paragraph Notes can help you organize facts from each paragraph of an article.**

Directions: Find at least one important fact from each paragraph of "Understanding Sumer." Record what you find on the chart below.

Paragraph-by-Paragraph Notes

Write one or more important facts from each paragraph here.

Paragraph #	Facts I found
1	Sumer is called the "birthplace" of civilization.
2	
3	
4	
5	
6	
7	
8	

© GREAT SOURCE. ALL RIGHTS RESERVED.

Understanding How History Textbooks Are Organized

Many history chapters open with a study guide or goals box. For example:

Study Guide

Main Idea: An area of Mesopotamia known as Sumer is considered the birthplace of civilization.

Goals: As you read, look for answers to these questions:

1. Where was Sumer located?
2. What problems did the earliest Sumerians face?
3. What was Uruk?
4. What important contributions did the Sumerians make to society?

Dates to Know

c. 5000 BC Ubaidian culture established in Sumer.

c. 4000 BC Uruk becomes Sumerian center of power. Sumerians invent wheel, ox-drawn plough, and writing.

Key Terms

nomads
city-states
surplus
polytheism
deity

Directions: Answer the questions under "Goals" in the Study Guide. Then define the key terms.

1. Where was Sumer located?

2. What problems did the earliest Sumerians face?

3. What was Uruk?

4. What important contributions did the Sumerians make to society?

Definitions of Key Terms

nomads

city-states

surplus

polytheism

deity

© GREAT SOURCE. ALL RIGHTS RESERVED.

NAME FOR USE WITH PAGES 66–83

E Connect

An excellent way of connecting to what you read is to imagine yourself a part of the action described.

- **Imagining yourself a part of a reading can help you make a strong connection to the text.**

Directions: Put yourself in a Sumerian farmer's shoes and answer these questions.

1. Why did you come to Sumer?

2. What is difficult about your life here?

After Reading

After you finish reading, take a moment to figure out how well you've understood the text.

F Pause and Reflect

Return to your 5 W's Organizer. Are there parts of the reading that you had trouble with?

- **Ask yourself, "How well did I meet my purpose?"**

Directions: Answer these two questions about "Understanding Sumer."

1. Which parts of the selection did you find easiest to understand?

2. Which were most challenging? Why?

© GREAT SOURCE. ALL RIGHTS RESERVED.

G Reread

The rereading strategy of outlining can help you get more from your second or third reading of a text.

• At the rereading stage, create an outline.

Directions: Complete this outline. Refer to your notes and the selection.

Outline

I. Early Sumerians

detail 1:

detail 2:

II. The Sumerian Religion

detail 1:

detail 2:

III. Sumerian Priests and Kings

detail 1:

detail 2:

H Remember

Sharing your ideas about what you have read can help you remember it.

• To remember what you have read, share what you learned.

Directions: Write three facts from the history text to share with a friend.

1.

2.

3.

© GREAT SOURCE. ALL RIGHTS RESERVED.

NAME

FOR USE WITH PAGES 84–99

Reading Geography

Your textbook is the key to unlocking important information about geography. Use your skills as a critical reader to help you get more from every chapter.

Before Reading

On the following pages, you'll practice using the reading process and the strategy of using graphic organizers with pages from a geography textbook. Take what you learn here and apply it to your own geography assignments.

A Set a Purpose

Your purpose for reading geography is to find out what the chapter or section is about and to learn why the information is important.

- **To set your purpose, turn the title into a question.**

Directions: Write your purpose for reading "Population Shift: Journey to Gold Mountain." Then predict what you think the reading will be about.

My purpose:

My predictions:

© GREAT SOURCE. ALL RIGHTS RESERVED.

B Preview

The reason you preview is so that you know what to expect during your close reading.

Directions: Preview "Population Shift: Journey to Gold Mountain." Make notes on the sticky notes.

Chapter 6

Population Shift
Journey to Gold Mountain

Preview

Key Terms

trade
emigrate
Gum Saan
immigrate
imperial
executed
barren

Places to Locate

Hong Kong
Canton
San Francisco

Read and Learn—

1. the reasons behind Chinese immigration to the U.S. in the nineteenth century.
2. travel conditions to Gold Mountain and beyond.
3. the challenges Chinese immigrants faced upon arriving in the U.S.

By the mid-1800s, **trade** between China and America was well established. Chinese sailors returning from America told of a land of great opportunity. Stories that America was "filled with treasures" spread from town to town and village to village. Soon, people were whispering that they wanted to **emigrate,** or move from, China.

Lure of Gold Mountain

News that gold had been discovered in 1848 in California made America seem all the more wonderful to the Chinese. In Canton, excitement about America reached a fevered pitch. Suddenly, the words ***Gum Saan***—which mean "Gold Mountain" in Chinese—were at the tip of everyone's tongue. Thousands of young Cantonese men began making secret plans to leave their homes and **immigrate,** or move to, California. (See the graph on the next page.)

The subject of the chapter: ....

....

....

....

....

Key terms to learn: ....

....

....

....

....

The first paragraph tells me: ....

....

....

....

....

© GREAT SOURCE. ALL RIGHTS RESERVED.

NAME FOR USE WITH PAGES 84–99

Textbooks

Approximate Number of Chinese Immigrants to California

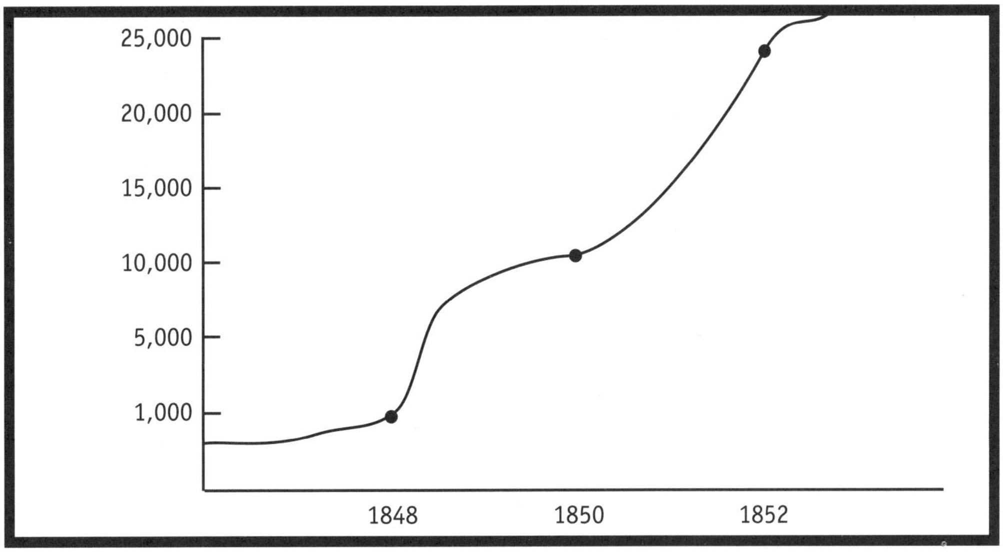

The need for secrecy was obvious. At the time, emigration from Canton—and all of China—was strictly forbidden. The Chinese **imperial** government, under the direction of an emperor, had decreed that any man caught leaving his home for work abroad was to be **executed,** or killed, on sight. So the young Cantonese men prepared for their journey under the cover of darkness and were unable to share their plans with anyone outside the immediate family.

Farewell to Canton

Most Cantonese families were thrilled to have a son, husband, or brother going to America. They understood the risks involved but viewed it as a golden opportunity to solve at least some of the problems that had plagued their families for generations. The land around Canton was rocky and **barren,** or bare. Farmers could only grow enough food to feed the population for four months out of the year. Starvation and disease were commonplace, and the Cantonese were desperate to improve their lives. Sending a relative to Gold Mountain seemed like a way to guarantee a whole family's survival.

I noticed this about the graphics:

© GREAT SOURCE. ALL RIGHTS RESERVED.

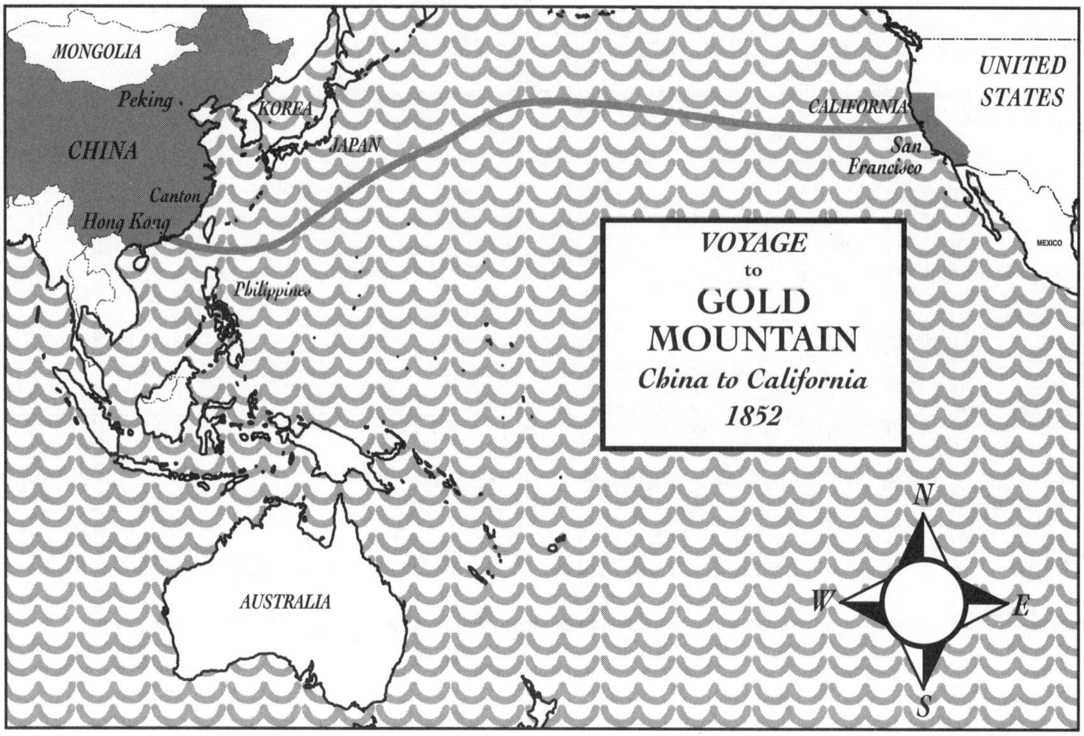

Shipping route from Hong Kong to San Francisco.

Passage to America

With their few belongings strapped to their backs, hordes of men boarded ships bound for America every week. Almost all were stowaways, hidden deep in the holds of the ship. The passage from Hong Kong to San Francisco took approximately three months. (See the map above.)

Most emigrants became ill during the long voyage, and some died. Those who had not brought enough food slowly starved. Rats and fleas plagued the healthy and sick alike. Halfway through the journey, most of the emigrants felt so miserable that they were sure they would die without ever seeing Gold Mountain. Night and day the ship's hold was filled with the sounds of men retching or crying from homesickness for their families and their beloved homeland.

Chinese workers digging for gold. (Circa 1855)

© GREAT SOURCE. ALL RIGHTS RESERVED.

NAME FOR USE WITH PAGES 84–99

C Plan

Next, make a plan. How can you find out what you need to know from this text? Graphic organizers can help.

- **Use graphic organizers to keep track of important information in a geography textbook.**

Directions: Complete this K-W-L Chart. In the left column, write what you already know about the Gold Rush. Write what you want to know in the middle column. Save the third column for later.

K-W-L Chart

What I Know	What I Want to Know	What I Learned

During Reading

Now go back and do a careful reading. Read slowly and think about the information. Ask yourself questions.

D Read with a Purpose

Remember to keep your reading purpose in mind. Your goal is to find out what the chapter or section is about and why this information is important.

© GREAT SOURCE. ALL RIGHTS RESERVED.

Using the Strategy

Many kinds of graphic organizers work well with geography textbooks. Your job as a critical reader is to choose the organizer that works best for you.

• You can use a Concept Map to help you explore a new term or concept.

Directions: Explore the term *emigration* on this Concept Map. Include details from the chapter and information you've learned on your own.

Concept Map

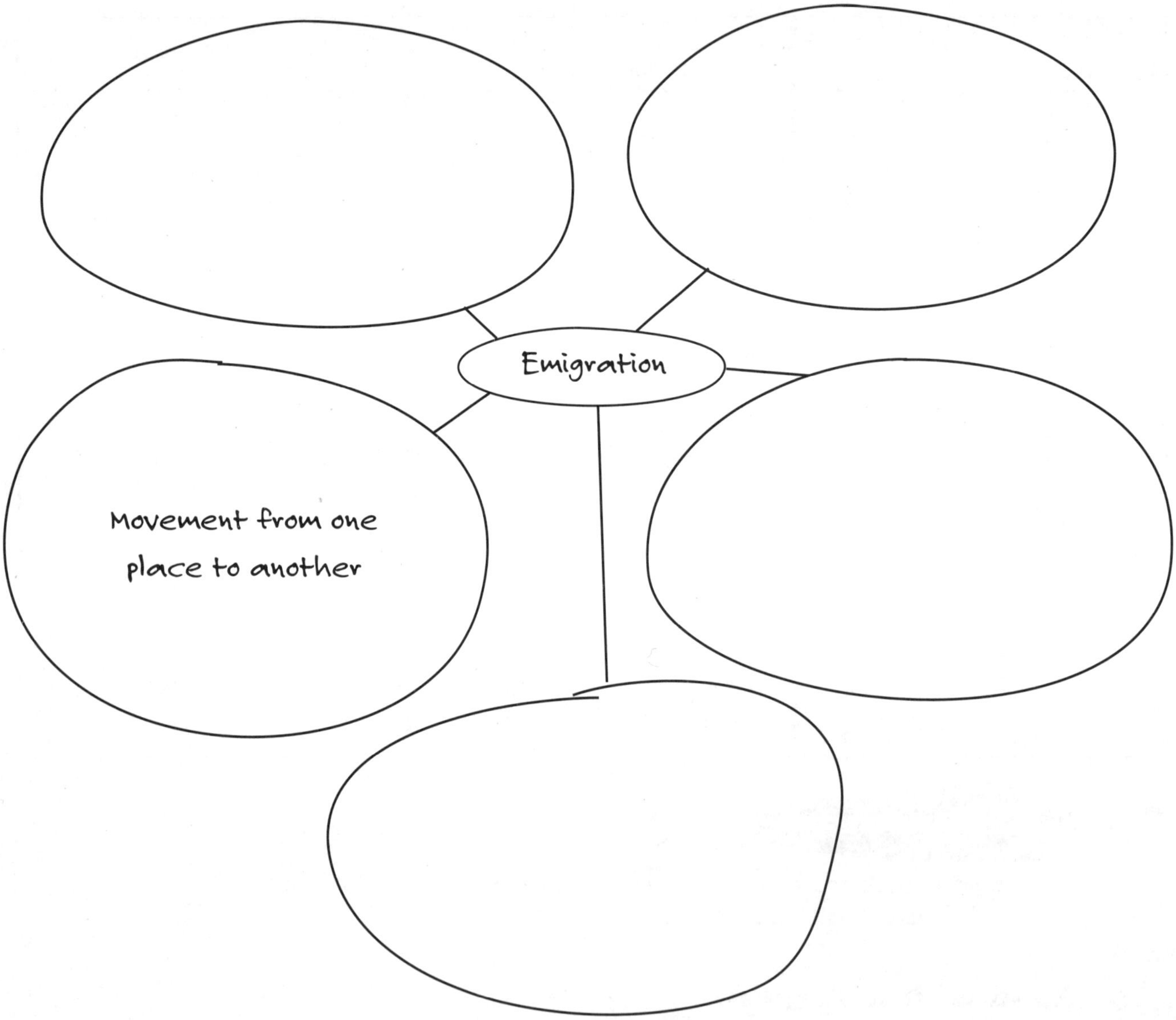

© GREAT SOURCE. ALL RIGHTS RESERVED.

NAME FOR USE WITH PAGES 84–99

Understanding How Geography Textbooks Are Organized

Topic Organization
Geography textbooks are usually organized around several key topics. Within each topic there are several subtopics or subpoints.

Directions: Look at the sample outline on page 94 of your handbook. Then complete this Topic Organization outline using notes from the "Journey to Gold Mountain" section of the chapter.

Topic Organization

I. Lure of Gold Mountain

A. detail 1

B. detail 2

II. Farewell to Canton

A. detail 1

B. detail 2

III. Passage to America

A. detail 1

B. detail 2

Use of Graphics
In addition to paying attention to key topics, you must also look carefully at the maps, graphs, tables, and photographs that appear throughout a geography textbook. Very often the point of a visual can be summed up in one sentence.

Directions: Look at the graph, map, and photo in "Journey to Gold Mountain." Write one sentence that summarizes the point of each visual.

One-sentence Summary

Graph:

Map:

Photo:

© GREAT SOURCE. ALL RIGHTS RESERVED.

E Connect

Making personal connections can help you understand and stay interested when you're reading a textbook.

- **As you read, make notes about information that you find interesting, surprising, or puzzling.**

Directions: Record your comments about the geography chapter here.

I was interested in these parts of the chapter: ....

....

I found this information surprising: ....

....

I'm puzzled by this: ....

....

After Reading

After you finish reading, take time to figure out what you learned.

F Pause and Reflect

Begin by reflecting on your reading purpose.

- **After you finish a geography chapter, ask yourself, "How well did I meet my purpose?"**

Directions: Return to the "L" section of your K-W-L Chart (page 33). Make notes about what you learned. Have you met your reading purpose? Circle *have* or *have not* below and explain.

I have / have not met my reading purpose. Here's why: ....

....

....

....

....

....

© GREAT SOURCE. ALL RIGHTS RESERVED.

NAME FOR USE WITH PAGES 84–99

G Reread

Even the best readers absorb only so much on a first reading. For this reason, it's a good idea to look back and reread.

- **A powerful rereading strategy to use is note-taking.**

Directions: Write a question about "Journey to Gold Mountain" on the front of each Study Card. Then exchange cards with a classmate and answer each other's questions.

Study Cards

Question: Why did the Chinese men keep their plans to emigrate a secret?

Answer:

Question:

Answer:

© GREAT SOURCE. ALL RIGHTS RESERVED.

H Remember

After you finish a reading, take time to make the material your own.

- **Creating a practice test can help you remember important information.**

Directions: Create a practice test that covers the material in the geography chapter. Then write an answer key.

Practice Test

"Population Shift: Journey to Gold Mountain"

1. What does "emigrate" mean?

a. move from a place   b. move to a place

c. look for a place to move   d. refuse to move

2.

a.   b.

c.   d.

3.

a.   b.

c.   d.

4.

a.   b.

c.   d.

5.

a.   b.

c.   d.

Answer Key

1.   2.   3.   4.   5.

© GREAT SOURCE. ALL RIGHTS RESERVED.

NAME .... FOR USE WITH PAGES 100–116

Reading Science

A science textbook teaches you to think like a scientist. Use the explanations, definitions, and charts to learn about science and how a scientist thinks. Practice reading and responding to a science text here.

Before Reading

Use the reading process and the strategy of note-taking to help you read and understand a section from a science chapter about earthquakes.

A Set a Purpose

Your purpose for reading science is to find out as much as you can about the subject. You'll also want to understand what the author is saying about it.

- **To set your purpose, ask a question about the subject and main idea of the section.**

Directions: Write your purpose for reading "Earthquakes" here. Then make a prediction. What do you expect to learn?

My purpose: ....

....

....

Here are three things I expect to learn: ....

1. ....

....

2. ....

....

3. ....

....

© GREAT SOURCE. ALL RIGHTS RESERVED.

B Preview

The title of a unit, chapter, or section can give you your first clue about the subject. The features on the checklist below will provide additional clues.

Preview Checklist

- [ ] headings
- [ ] boxed items
- [ ] words in boldface or repeated words
- [ ] any photos, maps, diagrams, and so on

Directions: Preview the science text pages that follow. Place a check beside each feature as you preview it. Then make some notes on the lines below.

The titles and headings tell me:

I noticed these boldface words:

The graphics tell me:

I expect to learn:

© GREAT SOURCE. ALL RIGHTS RESERVED.

NAME

FOR USE WITH PAGES 100–116

SECTION 3

Earthquakes

DISCOVER

- Learn what causes an earthquake.
- Learn what happens when an earthquake occurs.

RESEARCH

- Using the information you've gathered, create a 1-minute multimedia presentation about earthquakes in general or one earthquake in particular.
- Write a pamphlet entitled "Staying Safe During an Earthquake." Incorporate information from your textbook and your research.

GOALS

1. Find out about the Richter scale.
2. Learn about major earthquakes of the past.

Key Terms
fault lines
seismologist
Richter scale
seismograph

Tip for Reading
Keep a list of the characteristics of earthquakes. Refer to the list as you study for your next exam.

Very few natural phenomena can cause as much damage and generate as much hysteria as earthquakes. Over the centuries, earthquakes have been responsible for millions of deaths and untold amounts of damage to buildings, bridges, schools, homes, and all other kinds of property.

Causes of Earthquakes

No one is ever prepared for an earthquake, since there is no precise early warning system for this type of natural disaster. Earthquakes are sudden, violent shifting movements in the earth's crust. They can occur at any time and in any place, although some areas of the earth are more prone to earthquakes than others. Some earthquakes are quite small and go mostly unnoticed. Other earthquakes release more energy than a nuclear bomb blast.

Earthquakes are caused when the tectonic plates that make up the entire surface of the earth collide or scrape against one another. When this happens, the earth's surface shifts along the plate boundaries, called **fault lines.** Over a period of thousands

Damage caused by an earthquake in Hollywood, California, on January 17, 1994.

Textbooks

© GREAT SOURCE. ALL RIGHTS RESERVED.

of years, forces push at the rocks along a fault. When the force becomes too great, rocks break loose and slide past each other. The result is an earthquake.

Richter number	Description of earthquake	Average number per year
2.0–3.4	unnoticeable	800,000
3.5–4.2	barely felt	30,000
4.3–4.8	felt by most humans	4,800
4.9–5.4	felt by all	1,400
5.5–6.1	damaging	500
6.2–6.9	serious damage	100
7.0–7.3	very serious damage	15
7.4–8.0	catastrophic	4
8.0+	near total destruction	1

Figure 3.1 The Richter Scale

Measuring an Earthquake

Seismologists, the scientists who study earthquakes, use an instrument called a **Richter scale** to describe the intensity of an earthquake **(see Figure 3.1).** There is no upper limit on the Richter scale, but the largest shocks have had magnitudes in the 8.8 to 8.9 range.

To obtain a Richter scale measurement, seismologists use what is called a **seismograph.** A seismograph is an instrument that measures and records the strength with which the earth trembles during an earthquake. When shock waves pass through the earth, the seismograph records the movement on a sheet of paper. A seismograph is so sensitive that it can pick up movements from earthquakes thousands of miles away.

A seismograph, used by seismologists to measure the strength of an earthquake.

© GREAT SOURCE. ALL RIGHTS RESERVED.

NAME .... FOR USE WITH PAGES 100–116

When and Where Earthquakes Occur

Close to eighty percent of all earthquakes occur along the edge of the Pacific Plate. This area is called the Ring of Fire.

Of course, not all earthquakes occur at the Ring of Fire. In fact, close to 50,000 earthquakes large enough to be noticed without the aid of a seismograph occur each year over the entire earth. Of these 50,000 earthquakes, approximately 100 will cause substantial damage and loss of life. Catastrophic earthquakes occur at an average of one per year. The results can be devastating **(see Figure 3.2).**

Figure 3.2 Catastrophic Earthquakes Since 1906

Year	Place	Deaths	Richter Measurement
1906	San Francisco	503	8.3
1920	Gansu, China	100,000	8.6
1923	Yokohama, Japan	200,000	8.3
1927	Nan-Shan, China	200,000	8.3
1939	Chillan, Chile	40,000	8.3
1976	Tangshan, China	242,000	8.2
1985	Mexico City, Mexico	4,200	8.1

C Plan

After previewing the chapter, make a plan. Choose a strategy that can help you read, understand, and remember what you've learned about the subject.

- **Use the strategy of note-taking to get *more* from a science text.**

Before you begin reading, create a Thinking Tree. Use it to keep track of important facts and details from the reading.

© GREAT SOURCE. ALL RIGHTS RESERVED.

NAME

During Reading

Now do a careful reading of "Earthquakes." Write your notes on the Thinking Tree. Use the headings from the section as your guide to what's important.

Directions: Look at the sample Thinking Tree on page 107 of your handbook. Then use the Thinking Tree below for your notes from "Earthquakes."

Thinking Tree

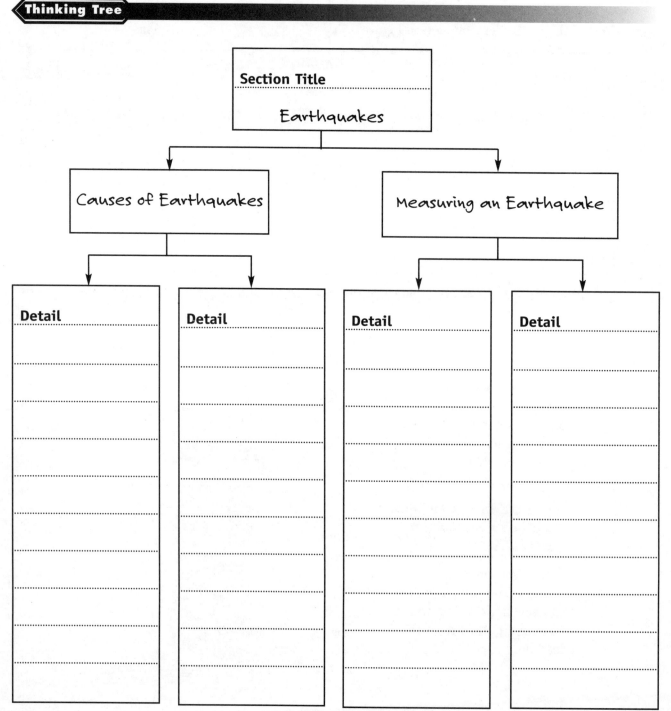

Section Title

Earthquakes

Causes of Earthquakes

Measuring an Earthquake

Detail

Detail

Detail

Detail

© GREAT SOURCE. ALL RIGHTS RESERVED.

NAME

FOR USE WITH PAGES 100–116

D Read with a Purpose

Remember that your purpose is to discover the subject and main idea. Use the note-taking strategy to help you get *more* information.

Using the Strategy

There are all different ways to take notes. Choose the method that's best for you. For example, you might decide to make Key Word Notes when reading science.

- **Use Key Word Notes to help you learn and remember key concepts in a reading.**

Directions: Complete this organizer. Refer to your notes from the reading.

Key Word Notes

Key Words / Concepts	Text Notes
fault lines	
seismologist	
catastrophic	

Textbooks

© GREAT SOURCE. ALL RIGHTS RESERVED.

Understanding How Science Texts Are Organized

Science textbook writers often use three important thought patterns: 1) cause-effect order, 2) classification order, and 3) problem-solution order.

Directions: Reread the information about seismographs. Think about how seismographs help scientists understand the problem of earthquakes. Make notes on this diagram.

Problem-Solution Order

Problem	Solution
Scientists want to learn more about	
earthquakes around the world.	

E Connect

Good readers consider how the information in a science chapter relates to them personally.

- **As you read, make notes about facts and details that you find interesting or puzzling.**

Directions: Write your reactions to the information about earthquakes here. What surprised you about the reading? What would you like to learn more about?

My reactions:

© GREAT SOURCE. ALL RIGHTS RESERVED.

NAME FOR USE WITH PAGES 100–116

After Reading

When you finish a reading in a science textbook, think about what you've learned.

F Pause and Reflect

Return to your reading purpose. Do you understand the subject and the main idea?

- **After you finish reading, ask yourself, "Did I meet my purpose?"**

Directions: Answer *yes* or *no* to these questions. All four relate to your reading purpose.

Checklist	Yes	No
1. Do I know the subject of the article?		
2. Do I understand what point the writer is making about the subject?		
3. Can I explain the key terms?		
4. Do the graphics, pictures, and captions make sense?		

G Reread

If you can't answer *yes* to each question, you probably need to do some rereading.

- **Use the strategy of skimming to help you answer specific questions.**

Directions: Write the most important idea about Richter scales in the Main Idea Organizer. Then skim for details that support this idea and write them in the organizer.

Main Idea Organizer

Subject: The Richter scale

Main idea:

Detail 1	Detail 2	Detail 3

© GREAT SOURCE. ALL RIGHTS RESERVED.

H Remember

There's more to science than what's in your textbook. Make the subject your own by talking about it with someone else.

- **Talking about a subject can help you remember it.**

Directions: Interview a family member about earthquakes. Write at least three interview questions beforehand.

Interview: Earthquakes

Question #1:

Answer:

Question #2:

Answer:

Question #3:

Answer:

© GREAT SOURCE. ALL RIGHTS RESERVED.

NAME FOR USE WITH PAGES 117–131

Reading Math

Math textbooks are brief and to the point. Every word, no matter how small or simple, counts for a whole lot. The key to reading math is recalling prior knowledge. Use what you already know to help you learn more.

Textbooks

Before Reading

Practice reading a math book here. Use the reading process and the strategy of visualizing and thinking aloud to help you get more out of a math text.

A Set a Purpose

Begin by setting your purpose. In most cases the subject is identified in the chapter title.

- **To set your purpose, turn the title of the chapter into a question.**

Directions: Write your purpose for reading the math chapter "Estimation and Mental Math." Then write what you think will be easiest and hardest about these pages.

My purpose:

The easiest part:

The hardest part:

© GREAT SOURCE. ALL RIGHTS RESERVED.

B Preview

It's very important that you preview a math text before you begin reading. Your preview can remind you of what you know and help you figure out what you need to learn.

• Use a K-W-L Chart for your preview notes.

Directions: Preview the following math pages. Pay attention to headings, boxed items, models, diagrams, and examples. Make some notes on this K-W-L Chart. Save the last column for after you have read.

K-W-L Chart

What I Know	What I Want to Know	What I Learned

© GREAT SOURCE. ALL RIGHTS RESERVED.

NAME .... FOR USE WITH PAGES 117-131

Math Feature

6

Estimation and Mental Math

What is the hottest place on earth? What is the coldest? Use estimation and mental math to help you explore weather around the world.

Materials

You will need Worksheet 6C.

Goal

Learn how to use estimation and mental math strategies.

Key Terms

front-end estimation

trading off

Front-end estimation is ....

1. For 43 consecutive days in July and August of 1917, air temperatures of over 120.2° were recorded in Death Valley, California. Find the mean of the four temperatures below.

120.8° 121.1° 120.3° 121.9°

Estimation Suppose you want to estimate the sum of the four temperatures. To estimate means to find an approximate answer. One way to estimate a sum is to use front-end estimation. **Front-end estimation** assumes that the left-most digits have the greatest value.

How the Strategy Works

When using front-end estimation, focus on the left-most digits.

Example

First add the front-end digits.	Next look at what is left.
120.8°	.8° } about 1
121.1°	.1°
120.3°	.3° } about 1
121.9°	.9°
120 + 121 + 120 + 121 = 482	About 2 more
My estimate:	The sum is more than 482.

© GREAT SOURCE. ALL RIGHTS RESERVED.

Then adjust your first estimate. 482° + 2° = 484°

The sum of the four temperatures is about 484°.

2. Use front-end estimation to estimate each sum.

a. 720 + 640 + 399 b. 6.98 + 4.01 + 17.54

c. 35.4 + 78.9 + 15.6 d. 9.18 + 30.02 + 20.9

Mental Math Mental math can help you find a sum. Use the strategy of **trading off**.

Use trading off to find the sum of three days of snowfall at Mt. Shasta Ski Bowl, California.

Trading off is

Add 3 to 97 to make it a round 100.

Day 1	97" + 3 ⟹		100"
Day 2	103" – 3 ⟹		100"
Day 3	107" + 3 ⟹	+	110"
		=	310"

Subtract 3 from 103 to make it a round 100.

Add 3 to 107 to make it a round 110.

3. Use trading off to find each sum.

a. 57 + 68 =

b. 217 + 33 =

c. 53 + 95 + 77 =

d. 193 + 208 =

e. 35 + 75 =

© GREAT SOURCE. ALL RIGHTS RESERVED.

NAME .... FOR USE WITH PAGES 117-131

C Plan

Your next step is to make a plan. Choose a strategy that can help you meet your reading purpose.

- **Use the strategy of thinking aloud to help you solve math equations and memorize formulas.**

During Reading

Now go back and do a careful reading of the two math pages. Use the strategy of thinking aloud to help you get more from the reading. Thinking aloud means talking yourself through a problem.

D Read with a Purpose

Keep in mind your purpose for reading. Remember that you want to learn about estimation and mental math. Make notes on the sticky notes.

Using the Strategy

Directions: On the lines below, write how you would use front-end estimation to solve this problem:

$$9.18 + 30.02 + 20.95 =$$

Think Aloud

© GREAT SOURCE. ALL RIGHTS RESERVED.

Understanding How Math Texts Are Organized

A math lesson usually will have an introduction with a study guide. For example:

After you finish a section or chapter, return to the box on the opening page. Check to see that you've met the goal and learned the key terms.

Directions: Fill out this box to show the structure of the lesson on pages 51 and 52. Make notes about the lesson parts.

Materials

You will need Worksheet 6C.

Goal

Learn how to use estimation and mental math strategies.

Key Terms

front-end estimation

trading off

1. Introduction, or opening explanation

2. Sample problems, front-end estimation

3. Exercises

© GREAT SOURCE. ALL RIGHTS RESERVED.

NAME FOR USE WITH PAGES 117-131

E Connect

You can make a math problem more interesting and easier to remember if you turn it into a situation you can relate to or an experience you've had. This is called making an analogy.

- **You can make a math problem feel more "real" if you make an analogy to your own life.**

Directions: Create an analogy for problem #2 on the chart. Use an event or experience from your own life.

Problem	Analogy
1. 60 mph x h = 240 miles h = number of hours	Well, my father drives 60 miles per hour, and Grandma's house is 240 miles away. How long does it take to get to her house?
2. 77 − n = 43	

Write your own analogy for the problem here.

© GREAT SOURCE. ALL RIGHTS RESERVED.

After Reading

When you finish reading, reflect on what you've learned.

F Pause and Reflect

Return to your reading purpose. Ask yourself what you've learned about estimation and mental math.

• At this point, ask yourself, "How well did I meet my purpose?"

Directions: Think about what you've learned. Check *yes* or *no* in response to each statement.

Checklist	Yes	No
I understand the key terms.		
I can explain what each term means.		
I understand the sample problems.		
I can take what I've learned and use it to solve the exercises.		

G Reread

If you cannot answer *yes* to every question on the checklist, you may need to return to the text and do some rereading.

• A powerful rereading strategy to use is note-taking.

Directions: Use the chart on the next page. Read the terms and concepts in the left column. Write definitions in the middle column and examples in the right column. One has been done for you.

© GREAT SOURCE. ALL RIGHTS RESERVED.

NAME FOR USE WITH PAGES 117-131

Key Terms	Definitions	Examples
estimation		
front-end estimation		
mental math	solving a problem in your head	$7 \times 6 = 42$
trading off		

H Remember

Many of the new math concepts you learn build on previous concepts.

- **Creating sample tests can help you retain what you've learned.**

Directions: Create a sample test that explores the strategy of front-end estimation or trading off. Give the test to a partner and see how well he or she does.

Sample Test

Strategy to Be Tested:

1. **2.**

3. **4.**

5. **6.**

7. **8.**

9. **10.**

© GREAT SOURCE. ALL RIGHTS RESERVED.

Focus on Science Concepts

In science and other subjects, concept *is a word for "big idea." Follow these steps to understand a science concept.*

Step 1: Learn key terms.

An important part of understanding science concepts is learning the definitions for key terms.

Directions: Look at the photosynthesis diagram below. Write key terms in the word bank. Use a dictionary to define each term.

Photosynthesis Diagram

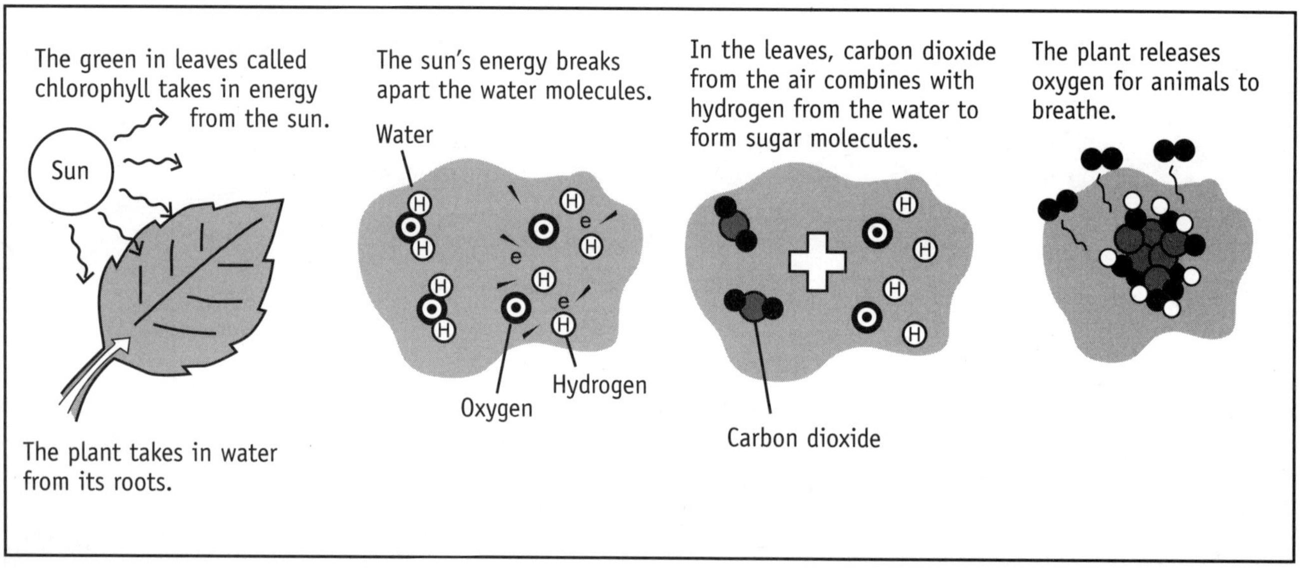
The green in leaves called chlorophyll takes in energy from the sun.
Sun
The plant takes in water from its roots.
The sun's energy breaks apart the water molecules.
Water
H
O
e
Oxygen
Hydrogen
In the leaves, carbon dioxide from the air combines with hydrogen from the water to form sugar molecules.
Carbon dioxide
The plant releases oxygen for animals to breathe.

Word Bank

© GREAT SOURCE. ALL RIGHTS RESERVED.

NAME .... FOR USE WITH PAGES 132–142

Step 2: Understand the steps in the process.

Your next step is to understand what's involved in the process. Making a Concept Map can help.

Directions: Write the steps in photosynthesis here. Include key terms from your word bank.

Concept Map

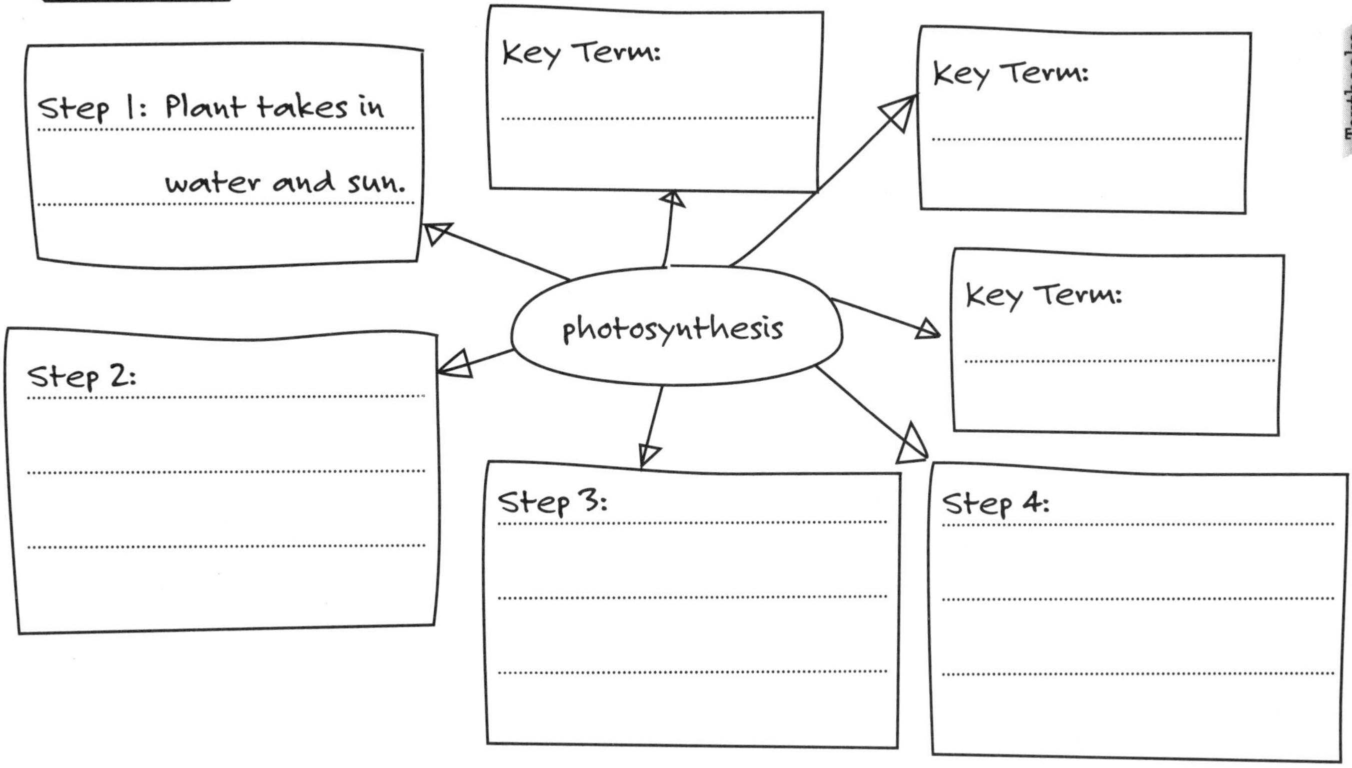

Step 3: Redraw or retell.

To make sure you fully understand a concept, explain it in your own words. Redraw the concept or tell what it's all about.

Directions: Look at the drawing on page 142 of your handbook. Then redraw photosynthesis in a similar way.

Drawing

© GREAT SOURCE. ALL RIGHTS RESERVED.

NAME

Focus on Word Problems

The good news about word problems is that they all are solved in pretty much the same way. You can follow this four-step plan.

Step 1: Read.

Begin by reading the problem a couple of times until you know what it is asking for.

Directions: Read this word problem. Take notes on the "topic," the "given," and the "unknown." Review page 144 of your handbook if you need help with these concepts.

Sample Question

1. Admission to Big Splash Water Park costs $22.00 for adults and $16.00 for children under 12. Jade and Rose Chavez want to take their three children, ages 6, 9, and 11, to the park. How much will the admission be for this family of 5?

Topic (what the problem is about):

What is given (important information about the topic):

What is unknown (what you need to find out):

© GREAT SOURCE. ALL RIGHTS RESERVED.

NAME .... FOR USE WITH PAGES 143–154

Step 2: Plan.

Next, choose your strategy. The strategy of visualizing works well with word problems.

Directions: Make a sketch that reflects the word problem on page 60.

Step 3: Solve.

Next, use your notes and sketch to write an equation that reflects the information in the problem.

Directions: Write an equation to solve the Big Splash Water Park problem.

My equation: ....

....

Step 4: Check.

Always check your work. The strategy of thinking aloud can help.

Directions: Write how you solved the problem.

Think Aloud

Let's see. I need to find out how much it will cost the Chavez family to go to the park.

....

....

....

....

© GREAT SOURCE. ALL RIGHTS RESERVED.

Reading an Essay

An essay can be lighthearted or serious, formal or informal. Some essays are intended to entertain and others to persuade or reveal an interesting idea. When you read an essay, do so with an ear to the words and an eye to the essayist's main idea.

Before Reading

Practice reading, responding to, and evaluating an essay here. Use the reading process and the strategy of outlining to help you get more from the essay "How to Eat a Guava."

A Set a Purpose

To set your purpose, ask a question. Focus on the title of the essay, the author, and what the author is saying about the subject.

- **Ask a question about the title, author, or author's message.**

Directions: Write your purpose-setting questions for reading "How to Eat a Guava."

My purpose: ....

© GREAT SOURCE. ALL RIGHTS RESERVED.

NAME

FOR USE WITH PAGES 172–187

B Preview

During your preview, watch for clues about the subject of the essay. Pay particular attention to the title, first paragraph, last paragraph, and any background information. Also watch for repeated words or phrases.

Directions: Preview "How to Eat a Guava." Write your preview notes on this Web.

Web

"How to Eat a Guava"

Author's name:

Essay subject:

Details from the first paragraph:

Details from the last paragraph:

Repeated or key words I noticed:

© GREAT SOURCE. ALL RIGHTS RESERVED.

"How to Eat a Guava" by Esmeralda Santiago

There are guavas at the Shop & Save. I pick one up the size of a tennis ball and finger the prickly stem end. It feels familiarly bumpy and firm. The guava is not quite ripe; the skin is still a dark green. I smell it and imagine a pale pink center, the seeds tightly embedded in the flesh.

A ripe guava is yellow, although some varieties have a pink tinge. The skin is thick, firm, and sweet. Its heart is bright pink and almost solid with seeds. The most delicious part of the guava surrounds the tiny seeds. If you don't know how to eat a guava, the seeds end up in the crevices between your teeth.

When you bite into a ripe guava, your teeth must grip the bumpy surface and sink into the thick edible skin without hitting the center. It takes experience to do this, as it's quite tricky to determine how far beyond the skin the seeds begin.

Stop and Record

Make some notes in the "Introduction" section of your outline (page 66).

Some years, when the rains have been plentiful and the nights cool, you can bite into a guava and not find many seeds. The guava bushes grow close to the ground, their branches laden with green then yellow fruit that seem to ripen overnight. These guavas are large and juicy, almost seedless, their roundness enticing you to have one more, just one more, because next year the rains may not come.

As children, we didn't always wait for the fruit to ripen. We raided the bushes as soon as the guavas were large enough to bend the branch.

A green guava is sour and hard. You bite into it at its widest point, because it's easier to grasp with your teeth. You hear the skin, meat, and seeds crunching inside your head, while the inside of your mouth explodes in little spurts of sour.

You grimace, your eyes water, and your cheeks disappear as your lips purse into a tight O. But you have another and then another, enjoying the crunchy sounds, the acid taste, the gritty texture of the unripe center. At night, your mother makes you drink castor oil, which she says tastes better than a green guava. That's when you know for sure that you're a child and she has stopped being one.

I had my last guava the day we left Puerto Rico. It was large and juicy, almost red in the center, and so fragrant that I didn't want to eat it because I would lose the smell. All the way to the airport I scratched at it with my teeth, making little dents in the skin, chewing small pieces with my front teeth, so that I could feel the texture against my tongue, the tiny pink pellets of sweet.

Stop and Record

Make some notes in the "Body" section of your outline (page 66).

© GREAT SOURCE. ALL RIGHTS RESERVED.

NAME .... FOR USE WITH PAGES 172–187

"How to Eat a Guava," continued

Today, I stand before a stack of dark green guavas, each perfectly round and hard, each $1.59. The one in my hand is tempting. It smells faintly of late summer afternoons and hopscotch under the mango tree. But it is autumn in New York, and I'm no longer a child.

The guava joins its sisters under the harsh fluorescent lights of the exotic fruit display. I push my cart away, toward the apples and pears of my adulthood, their nearly seedless ripeness predictable and bittersweet.

Stop and Record

Make some notes in the "Conclusion" section of your outline (page 66).

C Plan

What clues did you pick up from your preview of the essay? You probably can tell it is about guavas and how they taste. What do you already know about guavas? Put together your previous knowledge and what you picked up during your preview. This will give you an idea of the subject before you do a careful reading.

After your preview, make a plan for reading. Choose a strategy that can help you understand the essay.

- **The strategy of outlining can help you keep track of important details that relate to the author's thesis.**

© GREAT SOURCE. ALL RIGHTS RESERVED.

During Reading

Most essays contain three parts: an introduction, a body, and a conclusion. Make notes about each part as you read. Then use your notes to help you create your outline.

D Read with a Purpose

Remember that your purpose is to understand the writer's message, figure out the thesis, and decide how you feel about what is being said.

Directions: Do a careful reading of Esmeralda Santiago's essay. Watch for clues about her main idea in the concluding paragraph. Make notes on this outline as you read.

Sentence Outline

I. Introduction

A.

B.

II. Body

A.

B.

C.

III. Conclusion

A.

B.

© GREAT SOURCE. ALL RIGHTS RESERVED.

NAME

FOR USE WITH PAGES 172–187

Using the Strategy

It's important to include the essayist's thesis in your outline. If you can't figure out the thesis, use this formula:

subject + how the author feels about the subject = the author's thesis

Directions: Find the thesis of "How to Eat a Guava."

subject **+ how the author feels = thesis**

\+ =

Understanding How Essays Are Organized

Many essays follow one of several basic structures. Some essays tell a story and follow a chronological order. Other essays are developed around details that support a main idea or thesis statement. The main idea is often either in the first one or two paragraphs or the last paragraph.

- **Use a graphic to help you figure out how an essay is organized.**

Directions: Complete this organizer. Explain what the writer describes in the introduction and body of the essay. Then write a sentence about the conclusion with the implied main idea in "How to Eat a Guava."

Essay Organizer

introduction

body

conclusion

with main idea

© GREAT SOURCE. ALL RIGHTS RESERVED.

A Main Idea Organizer is another way of making sense of what the author is saying.

Directions: Complete the Main Idea Organizer for "How to Eat a Guava."

Main Idea Organizer

TITLE:		
MAIN IDEA:		
DETAIL #1	DETAIL #2	DETAIL #3
CONCLUSION:		

E Connect

Making personal connections to the essayist's subject and message can help you meet your reading purpose.

- **Connect to an essay by recording your thoughts and feelings about the subject.**

Directions: Think of a vivid childhood memory—one that you can see, hear, smell, and taste. Describe it here.

© GREAT SOURCE. ALL RIGHTS RESERVED.

NAME

FOR USE WITH PAGES 172–187

After Reading

After you finish reading, think back to your reading purpose.

F Pause and Reflect

Decide whether you understand the subject and thesis.

- **Ask yourself, "How well did I meet my purpose?"**

Directions: Answer these questions about "How to Eat a Guava."

What is the subject of the essay?

What is the author's thesis?

How do you feel about the author's message?

Would you say you've met your reading purpose? Why or why not?

© GREAT SOURCE. ALL RIGHTS RESERVED.

G Reread

Do you have lingering questions about the essay? If so, choose a strategy that can help you find answers.

- **A powerful rereading strategy to use is questioning the author.**

Directions: Write three questions for Esmeralda Santiago. Then write what you imagine her answers would be.

Question #1:

Santiago's answer:

Question #2:

Santiago's answer:

Question #3:

Santiago's answer:

© GREAT SOURCE. ALL RIGHTS RESERVED.

NAME FOR USE WITH PAGES 172–187

H Remember

Good readers retain what they've read.

- **Writing a summary can help you remember what you've read.**

Directions: Write a summary of "How to Eat a Guava." Be sure to include Santiago's message and an analysis of how the essay made you feel.

My Summary of "How to Eat a Guava"

© GREAT SOURCE. ALL RIGHTS RESERVED.

Nonfiction

Reading a Biography

A biography is the story of someone's life. Most biographers write with two goals in mind:

1. They want to tell an interesting story about the events in a person's life.

2. They want to create a "portrait," or impression, of that person so that readers can understand what he or she was like.

Before Reading

Practice using the reading process and the strategy of looking for cause and effect with this passage from a biography about Sadako Sasaki, a Japanese girl who folded one thousand paper cranes before dying of leukemia, the so-called "Atomic Bomb" disease.

A Set a Purpose

When reading a biography, your purpose is to find information about the biographical subject so that you can form an impression of him or her.

- **To set your purpose, ask a question about the biographical subject.**

Directions: Write your purpose for reading a biography about Sadako. Then tell what you already know about her.

My purpose: ....

....

....

....

Here's what I already know about Sadako: ....

....

....

....

© GREAT SOURCE. ALL RIGHTS RESERVED.

NAME

FOR USE WITH PAGES 188–203

B Preview

Next, preview the text. Pay particular attention to any introductory pages.

Directions: Skim the two introductory pages to Sadako's biography. Make notes on the lines below.

Who is the subject of the biography?

What is the main time period of the biography?

How do you know?

What did you learn from the introductory text?

What did you notice about the introductory art?

What is the title of the biography?

Who is the author?

What did you learn from the first paragraph of text?

© GREAT SOURCE. ALL RIGHTS RESERVED.

Introduction

One Thousand Paper Cranes

The Story of Sadako

In Japan, the crane is known as the "bird of happiness." According to the story, one crane equals a thousand years of happiness. Cranes are also a symbol of long life and good health. For this reason, they are a popular gift for those who are ill.

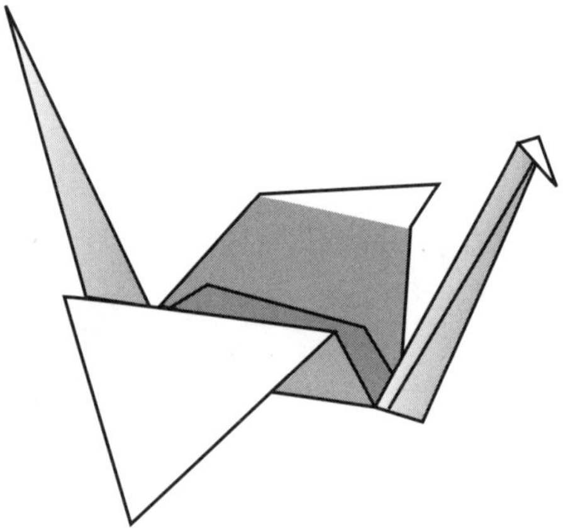

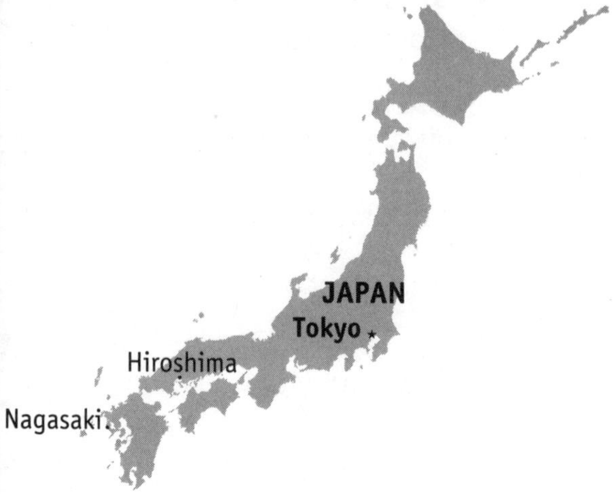

Sadako Sasaki was two years old when the U.S. dropped an atomic bomb on Hiroshima on August 6, 1945. Ten years later, Sadako died of "Atomic Bomb" disease. Before she died, Sadako declared that she would fold one thousand paper cranes as a symbol of her hope for peace. After her death, the children in Sadako's class worked with others to fold paper cranes and build the Children's Peace Statue in memory of Sadako and the many children who were victims of the bombing of Hiroshima.

C Plan

Next make a plan. As you read, look for "life-shaping" events in the subject's life. These can help you understand the subject's personality.

- **Use the strategy of looking for cause and effect.**

© GREAT SOURCE. ALL RIGHTS RESERVED.

NAME

FOR USE WITH PAGES 188–203

During Reading

Now do a careful reading of the excerpt. Take notes about key events as you go.

D Read with a Purpose

Also keep in mind your purpose. Remember that you want to form an impression of the biographical subject.

Directions: Fill out the "Causes/Events" side of this Cause-Effect Organizer as you read. You'll return to the "Effect" box later.

Cause-Effect Organizer

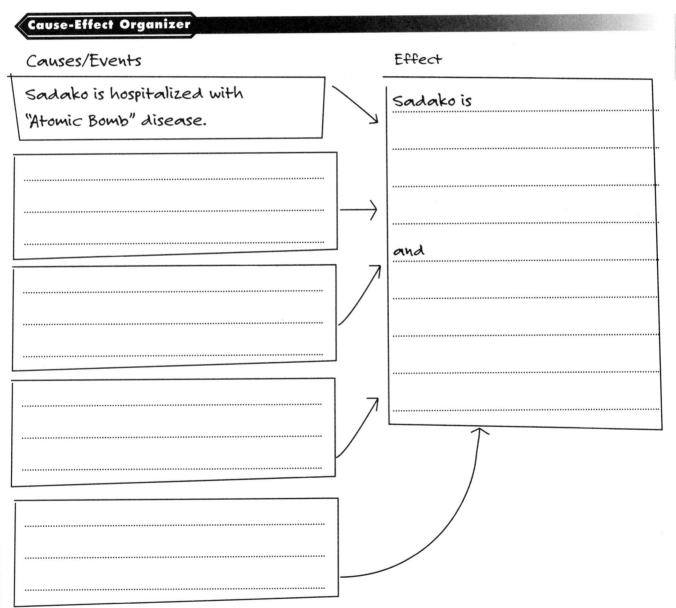

Causes/Events

Sadako is hospitalized with "Atomic Bomb" disease.

Effect

Sadako is

and

© GREAT SOURCE. ALL RIGHTS RESERVED.

Chapter 4 Folding Paper Cranes

A few days after the Peace Ceremony, a nurse came into Sadako's room, carrying a chain of folded paper cranes. "Look Sadako, aren't these pretty? A girl from a high school in Nagoya sent hundreds of them to our patients. I thought you and Kiyo might like to have these paper cranes." Sadako and Kiyo were very happy to get them. Sadako remembered a story which her mother had told her several years ago: if you fold a thousand paper cranes, your wish will come true. So Sadako said to Kiyo, "*One-e-chan*, let's fold paper cranes!" "Okay," said Kiyo, and together they started on their new project of folding paper cranes.

At first they used any kind of paper they could find, but eventually they settled on the square sheets of paper used by the hospital to wrap powdered medicines.

"I will fold one thousand cranes, starting right here and now," said a determined Sadako.

Now Sadako had a mission. She would fold a thousand paper cranes all by herself and her wish would be granted. Sitting straight up in bed she vigorously folded the cranes. She was determined not to let anything stop her from reaching her goal. It soon became evident that a single source of paper would not be enough for her to achieve her goal, so she doggedly searched for every piece of paper she could find, including scraps of candy wrappers and gift wrap. Sadako had placed her chains of folded cranes all over her room, hanging down from the ceiling.

Stop and Record

What important events have you read about so far? Make notes on your Cause-Effect Organizer. ***(page 75).***

"Sadako, you fold cranes very nicely and so very fast!" said Kiyo.

Sadako replied, "I must fold them. I've got to finish a thousand of them if I'm going to get better."

There were days when Sadako wasn't feeling well, but she continued faithfully to fold the cranes.

During one of his visits in mid-August, Mr. Sasaki noticed how pale and drawn his daughter looked. "Sadako, you look so tired. Why don't you put aside the cranes and rest?"

"It's okay, Papa. I have a reason for folding them. If I finish folding a thousand of them, I believe that my wish to be healthy again will come true."

Unfortunately, as time passed and the number of cranes grew larger, Sadako's condition did not improve, and her pain and discomfort increased. In spite of this, Sadako continued folding the cranes with her resolute belief that she would get better.

© GREAT SOURCE. ALL RIGHTS RESERVED.

NAME

FOR USE WITH PAGES 188–203

Using the Strategy

As you read, form your own impression of the biographical subject. Also think carefully about the "portrait" the writer has created.

Directions: Return to the "Effect" side of the Cause-Effect Organizer on page 75. Write two adjectives (descriptive words) that describe Sadako. Refer to your preview and during-reading notes as needed.

Understanding How Biographies Are Organized

Besides paying attention to facts about important events, you should also look for details about what the biographical subject was like. A Character Map can help.

Directions: Make notes about Sadako on this Character Map.

Character Map

What the character says	How the character acts and feels
Sadako	
What others think about her	How I feel about her

© GREAT SOURCE. ALL RIGHTS RESERVED.

E Connect

To connect with a biography, consider your own feelings about the biographical subject.

- **Record your own thoughts and feelings as you read.**

Directions: Tell why you feel the way you do about Sadako.

I think Sadako is

because

After Reading

After you finish reading, think about what you've learned.

F Pause and Reflect

At this point, you'll want to return to your reading purpose.

- **To reflect on your purpose, ask yourself, "Do I know enough to tell someone about this biography?"**

Directions: Complete this chart. If you have trouble, do some rereading.

Three important events in Sadako's life:	What she was like:
1.	
2.	
3.	

© GREAT SOURCE. ALL RIGHTS RESERVED.

NAME

FOR USE WITH PAGES 188–203

G Reread

If you haven't yet formed an impression of the subject, you may need to do some rereading.

- **The strategy of outlining can help you get *more* from your rereading.**

Directions: Take another look at the excerpt. Make notes on this Outline.

Outline

Sadako Sasaki

I. Early Years

A. important event: Hiroshima is bombed.

B. important event: Sadako's family rebuilds their lives.

II. School-age Years

A. important event:

B. important event:

C. important event:

H Remember

Do your best to remember the most important details of a biography.

- **Use Study Cards to help you retain what you've learned.**

Directions: Complete this Study Card about Sadako Sasaki. Write important details from the reading.

Study Card

Sadako Sasaki

© GREAT SOURCE. ALL RIGHTS RESERVED.

Nonfiction

Reading an Autobiography

In autobiographies, writers tell the story of their own lives. Most autobiographers have two goals in mind. They want to tell their life story in an interesting or dramatic way, and they want to create a flattering self-portrait that readers can relate to and admire.

Before Reading

As a critical reader, your job is to learn the author's story and then respond to his or her self-portrait. Use the reading process and strategy of synthesizing to help you read and understand one of the great autobiographies of the world, *The Autobiography of Benjamin Franklin.*

A Set a Purpose

Look for answers to these two questions as you read: "What kind of life did the autobiographer have?" and "How do I feel about him or her?"

- **To set your purpose, ask two questions about the autobiographer.**

Directions: Write two questions about *The Autobiography of Benjamin Franklin.* Finding answers will be your purpose.

My Purpose, Question #1:

My Purpose, Question #2:

© GREAT SOURCE. ALL RIGHTS RESERVED.

NAME .... FOR USE WITH PAGES 204-217

B Preview

After you set your purpose, preview the autobiography. Look carefully at the front and back covers of the book. What do you learn?

Directions: Preview the front and back covers of *The Autobiography of Benjamin Franklin*. Write important information on the sticky notes.

Back Cover

Learn about the life and times of Ben Franklin, American printer, publisher, inventor, and scientist.

Dear Son:

I have ever had pleasure in obtaining any little anecdotes of my ancestors. Imagining it may be equally agreeable to you to know the circumstances of my life . . . I sit down to write them for you.

1706–1790

—Benjamin Franklin, to his son

Front Cover

The Autobiography of Benjamin Franklin

by **Benjamin Franklin**

Nonfiction

Important details

detail #1 ....

....

detail #2 ....

....

detail #3 ....

....

The title

....

....

The author

....

....

© GREAT SOURCE. ALL RIGHTS RESERVED.

NAME

C Plan

When you've finished previewing, make a reading plan that can help you meet your reading purpose. The strategy of synthesizing can help. Synthesizing is like gathering up the pieces of a puzzle and figuring out how they fit together.

- **Use the strategy of synthesizing to help you see the full picture of the autobiographer's life.**

Directions: Use the Key Topic Organizer for your synthesizing notes. Read the key topics in the left column. In the right column write notes.

Key Topic Organizer

Key Topics	Notes from Reading
childhood	
family	
school	
work	

© GREAT SOURCE. ALL RIGHTS RESERVED.

NAME .... FOR USE WITH PAGES 204-217

During Reading

Now do a careful reading of Ben Franklin's story. As you read, make notes in the Key Topic Organizer.

D Read with a Purpose

Keep in mind your reading purpose. Remember that you are looking for information about Ben Franklin's life. Also decide how you feel about him.

from *The Autobiography of Benjamin Franklin* by Benjamin Franklin

Josiah, my father, married young, and carried his wife with three children into New England, about 1682. . . . By the same wife he had four children more born there, and by a second wife ten more, in all seventeen; of which I remember thirteen sitting at one time at his table, who all grew up to be men and women, and married; I was the youngest son, and the youngest child but two, and was born in Boston, New England. My mother, the second wife, was Abiah Folger, daughter of Peter Folger, one of the first settlers of New England. . . .

My elder brothers were all put apprentices to different trades. I was put to the grammar school at eight years of age, my father intending to devote me, as the tithe of his sons, to the service of the Church. My early readiness in learning to read (which must have been very early, as I do not remember when I could not read), and the opinion of all his friends, that I should certainly make a good scholar, encouraged him in this purpose of his. My uncle Benjamin, too, approved of it, and proposed to give me all his shorthand volumes of sermons, I suppose as a stock to set up with, if I would learn his character. I continued, however, at the grammar school not quite one year, though in that time I had risen gradually from the middle of the class of that year to be the head of it, and farther was removed into the next class above it, in order to go with that into the third at the end of the year. But my father, in the meantime, from a view of the expense of a college education, which having so large a family he could not well afford, and the mean living many so educated were afterwards able to obtain—reasons that he gave to his friends in my hearing—altered his first intention, took me from the grammar school, and sent me to a school for writing and arithmetic, kept by a then famous man, Mr. George Brownell, very successful in his profession generally, and that by mild, encouraging methods. Under him I acquired fair writing pretty soon, but I failed in the arithmetic, and made no progress in it.

Nonfiction

© GREAT SOURCE. ALL RIGHTS RESERVED.

At ten years old I was taken home to assist my father in his business, which was that of a tallow chandler and soap boiler; a business he was not bred to, but had assumed on his arrival in New England, and on finding his dying trade would not maintain his family, being in little request. Accordingly, I was employed in cutting wick for the candles, filling the dipping mold and the molds for cast candles, attending the shop, going of errands, etc.

Stop and Record

Make notes on your Key Topic Organizer about Franklin's family, childhood, and school years. (page 82). What kind of a child was Ben Franklin?

I disliked the trade, and had a strong inclination for the sea, but my father declared against it; however, living near the water, I was much in and about it, learned early to swim well, and to manage boats; and when in a boat or canoe with other boys, I was commonly allowed to govern, especially in any case of difficulty; and upon other occasions I was generally a leader among the boys, and sometimes led them into scrapes, of which I will mention one instance, as it shows an early projecting public spirit, tho' not then justly conducted.

There was a salt marsh that bounded part of the millpond, on the edge of which, at high water, we used to stand to fish for minnows. By much trampling, we had made it a mere quagmire. My proposal was to build a wharf there fit for us to stand upon, and I showed my comrades a large heap of stones, which were intended for a new house near the marsh, and which would very well suit our purpose. Accordingly, in the evening, when the workmen were gone, I assembled a number of my play fellows, and working with them diligently like so many emmets,* sometimes two or three to a stone, we brought them all away and built our little wharf. The next morning the workmen were surprised at missing the stones, which were found in our wharf. Inquiry was made after the removers; we were discovered and complained of; several of us were corrected by our fathers; and though I pleaded the usefulness of the work, mine convinced me that nothing was useful which was not honest.

* An *emmet* is an ant.

Stop and Record

Return to your Key Topic Organizer (page 82). Make some notes about Franklin's work experience.

© GREAT SOURCE. ALL RIGHTS RESERVED.

NAME FOR USE WITH PAGES 204-217

Using the Strategy

When you synthesize, you examine individual topics or ideas in a reading and then see how they all work together.

• Use a Character Trait Web to zero in on one or two key topics.

Directions: Complete a Character Trait Web about Ben Franklin. Find details from the autobiography that are proof of each trait.

Character Trait Web

BEN FRANKLIN

Trait: Hard-working

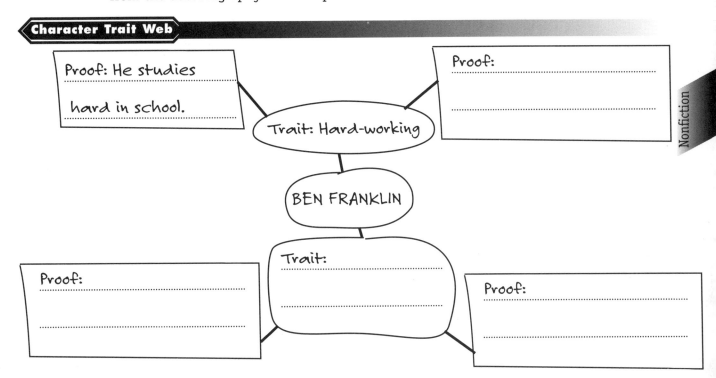

Proof: He studies hard in school.

Proof:

Trait:

Proof:

Proof:

Understanding How Autobiographies Are Organized

Autobiographers often use chronological (time) order to tell the story of their lives. You can use a Timeline to track major events in the writer's life.

Directions: Complete the Timeline. Write one event in each box.

Timeline

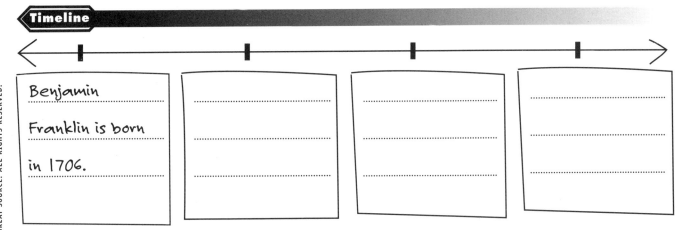

Benjamin Franklin is born in 1706.			

© GREAT SOURCE. ALL RIGHTS RESERVED.

E Connect

Remember that a part of your purpose is to decide how you feel about the autobiographer. An Inference Chart can help you put your ideas into words.

- **Record your impressions, or how you feel, about the autobiographer.**

Inference Chart

What Ben Franklin said or did	My feelings about him
• He rose to the head of his class. • He failed arithmetic when he was ten.	He was very bright, even as a child.
• He says he disliked the candle-making business.	
• He wanted to go to sea.	
• He built a wharf with his friends and got in trouble.	

© GREAT SOURCE. ALL RIGHTS RESERVED.

NAME .... FOR USE WITH PAGES 204-217

After Reading

After you finish an autobiography, think about the self-portrait the writer has created.

F Pause and Reflect

Take a moment to reflect on what you've learned.

- **After you finish reading, put together what you've learned about the autobiographer.**

Directions: Answer these three questions about Ben Franklin. Refer to your notes as needed.

What are three important events in Ben Franklin's life?

What kind of life did he have? Explain your answer.

How do you feel about him? Why?

Nonfiction

© GREAT SOURCE. ALL RIGHTS RESERVED.

G Reread

If you aren't sure of how you feel about Ben Franklin, you may need to do some rereading. As you reread, look for the events that shaped his personality.

- **Looking for cause and effect can help you track the events that shaped the writer's personality.**

Directions: Think about the events that helped Franklin become a famous American printer, publisher, inventor, and scientist. List some of these "causes" on the organizer below.

Cause-Effect Organizer

CAUSES

As a child, he enjoyed writing.

EFFECT

Franklin becomes a famous American printer, publisher, inventor, and scientist.

© GREAT SOURCE. ALL RIGHTS RESERVED.

NAME

FOR USE WITH PAGES 204-217

H Remember

It's important to remember what you've read. Writing your opinion can help.

- **Writing your opinion can help you remember what you've read.**

Directions: Write your opinion of *The Autobiography of Benjamin Franklin.* Be sure to explain your ideas.

Journal

This is what I liked best about Ben Franklin's autobiography:

because

This is what I did not like:

because

Nonfiction

© GREAT SOURCE. ALL RIGHTS RESERVED.

Reading a Newspaper Article

People read newspaper articles to find out what's happening in their world. You can use the reading process to get more from every article you read.

Before Reading

Because the reading process helps you evaluate information and form your own opinions about what you are reading, it is useful when you read newspaper articles. Practice using the reading process and the strategy of reading critically with the account that follows about a terrible fire.

A Set a Purpose

Your general purpose for reading a newspaper article is to find out what it has to say about the subject.

- **To set your purpose, take several words from the headline and use them in a question.**

Directions: Write your purpose for reading "Fire at a New York Shirtwaist Factory" below. Try to include at least two questions.

My purpose:

© GREAT SOURCE. ALL RIGHTS RESERVED.

NAME .... FOR USE WITH PAGES 218-233

B Preview

Newspaper articles are written for people who are in a hurry. That's why the lead (the first few paragraphs) of an article is so important.

Directions: Read the headnote and first two paragraphs of the article that follows. Then complete as much of this 5 W's Organizer as you can.

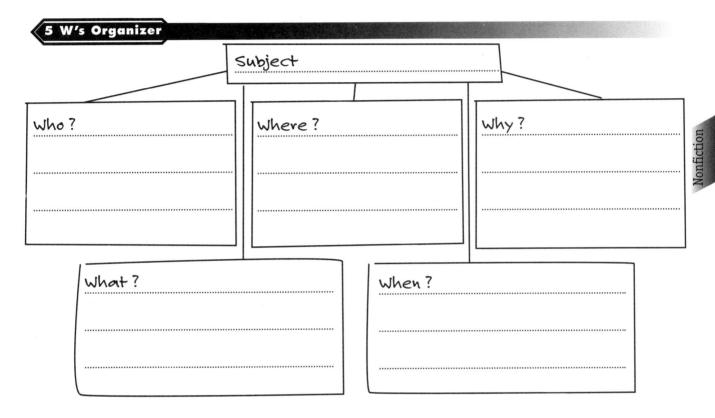

5 W's Organizer

Subject ....

Who? ....

Where? ....

Why? ....

What? ....

When? ....

"Fire at a New York Shirtwaist Factory" by W. G. Shepherd

What follows is a famous newspaper article about the Triangle Shirtwaist Factory fire in March of 1911. This article was originally published in the Cleveland Press *two days after the fire in which 146 people lost their lives.*

NEW YORK, March 27, 1911—I was walking through Washington Square when a puff of smoke issuing from the factory building caught my eye. I reached the building before the alarm was turned in. I saw every feature of the tragedy visible from outside the building. I learned a new sound—a more horrible sound than description can picture. It was the thud of a speeding, living body on a stone sidewalk.

Thud—dead! Thud—dead! Thud—dead! Thud—dead! Sixty-two! The sound and the thought of death came to me, each time, at the same instant. There was plenty of chance to watch them as they came down; the height was 80 feet.

© GREAT SOURCE. ALL RIGHTS RESERVED.

C Plan

Next make a plan. Choose a reading strategy that can help you answer these important questions: *who, what, where, when,* and *why.*

• Use the strategy of reading critically with newspaper articles.

Directions: Make notes on this Critical Reading Chart as you read Shepherd's article.

Critical Reading Chart

These are the questions you should ask yourself while reading a newspaper article.

Questions	My Thoughts
What are facts and what are opinions?	
Is the reporter's opinion well supported by evidence?	
Are the sources authoritative and reliable?	
What's the other side of the story?	

During Reading

Now do a careful reading of W. G. Shepherd's article.

D Read with a Purpose

Use your Critical Reading Chart to help you separate facts from opinions. As you read the rest of W. G. Shepherd's article, think about your reading purpose. What subject do you need to find out about?

© GREAT SOURCE. ALL RIGHTS RESERVED.

NAME FOR USE WITH PAGES 218-233

"Fire at a New York Shirtwaist Factory" by W. G. Shepherd, continued

The first 10 shocked me. I looked up, saw that there were scores of girls in the windows. The flames from the floor below were beating into their faces. Somehow I knew that they, too, would just come down, and something within me—something that I didn't know was there—steeled me.

I even watched one girl falling. She, waving her arms, tried to keep her body upright. Until the very instant she touched the sidewalk, she was trying to balance herself. Then came the thud—then a silent, unmoving pile of clothing and twisted, broken limbs.

As I reached the scene of the fire, a mushroom of smoke hung over the 10-story building. I glanced up and on the edge of the roof saw a young man walking along with his overcoat over his arm. He appeared to be waiting for the fire engines. But none was there. There was none even in sight or within hearing.

I noticed that the man was well dressed and had a jaunty air. His hands were in his trousers pockets. Five minutes later I saw him jump out into space. His overcoat parachuted in the air beside him. A moment later he was lifeless on the sidewalk.

I looked up to the seventh floor. There was a living picture in each window—four screaming girls, waving their arms. "Call the firemen," they screamed—scores of them. "Get a ladder," cried others. They were all as alive and whole and sound as were we who stood on the sidewalk: I couldn't help thinking of that. We cried to them not to jump. We heard the siren of a fire engine in some distant block. Then other sirens sounded from several directions.

"Here they come!" we yelled. "Don't jump! Stay there!"

One girl climbed onto a window sash. Those behind her tried to hold her back. Then she dropped into space. I didn't notice whether those above watched her drop. I turned away. Then came that first thud—dead impression.

Stop and Record

What are the facts of this fire? Record them on your Critical Reading Chart (page 92).

I looked up. Another girl was climbing onto the window sill. Others were crowding behind her. She dropped. I watched her fall and heard the sound. Two windows away two girls were climbing onto the sill. They were fighting and crowding each other for air. Behind them I saw many screaming heads. They fell, almost together. But I heard two distinct thuds.

Suddenly the flames broke out through the windows on the floor below them, and curled up into their faces. The firemen began to raise a ladder. Others took out life

Nonfiction

© GREAT SOURCE. ALL RIGHTS RESERVED.

nets. While they were rushing to the sidewalk with them two more girls shot down. The firemen held the net under the bodies. The two bodies broke it. The grotesque simile of a dog jumping through a paper hoop struck me. Before they could move the net another girl's body flashed into it.

The thuds were just as loud, it seemed, as if there had been no net there. It seemed to me that the thuds were so loud that they might have been heard all over the city, like dull explosion roars.

I had counted 10. Then my dulled sense began to work automatically. I noticed things that it had not occurred to me before to notice, little details that the first shock had blinded me to. I looked up to see whether those above watched those who fell. I noticed that they did—watched them every inch of the way down and probably heard the roaring thuds that we heard, unless the roaring flames were too loud.

As I looked up I saw a love affair in the midst of all the horror. A young man at a window helped a girl to the window sill; then he held her out, deliberately, away from the building, and let her drop. He seemed cool and calculating. He held out a second girl in the same way and then let her drop. Then he held out a third girl. They didn't resist. I noticed that they were as unresisting as if he was helping them onto a street car instead of into eternity.

Undoubtedly he saw that a terrible death awaited them in the flames and his aid was only a terrible chivalry.

Then came love amid the flames. He brought another girl to the window. Those of us who were looking saw him put her arms about him and kiss him. Then he held her out into space and dropped her. But, quick as a flash he was on the window sill himself. His coat flattened upward: the air filled his trouser legs; I could see that he wore tan shoes, and hose. His hat remained on his head.

Thud—dead! Thud—dead! They went into eternity together. I saw his face before they covered it. You could see in it that he was a real man. He had done his best.

We found out later that, in the room in which he stood, many girls were being burned to death by the flames, and were screaming in an inferno of heat and smoke. He chose the easiest way and was brave enough even to help the girl he loved to die, after she had given him a goodbye kiss. He leaped with energy as if he believed that he could cheat gravity and arrive first in that mysterious land of eternity only a second of time distant, to receive her. But her thud—dead! came first.

Stop and Record

How does the reporter feel about the fire? Record his opinion on your Critical Reading Chart (page 92).

© GREAT SOURCE. ALL RIGHTS RESERVED.

NAME FOR USE WITH PAGES 218-233

"Fire at a New York Shirtwaist Factory" by W. G. Shepherd, continued

The firemen raised their ladder. It reached only to the sixth floor. I saw the last girl jump at it and miss it. And then the faces disappeared from the windows.

By now the crowd was large, though all this had occurred in less than seven minutes—the start of the fire and the thuds and deaths. I heard screams around the corner and hurried there. What I had seen before was not so terrible as what followed.

Girls were burning to death before our eyes. There were jams in the windows. No one was lucky enough to be able to jump, it seemed. But, one by one, the jams broke. Down came bodies in a shower, burning, smoking, lighted bodies, with the disheveled hair of the girls trailing upward. They had fought each other to die by jumping instead of by fire.

There were 33 in that shower. The flesh of some of them was cooked. The clothes of most of them were burned away. The whole, sound, unharmed girls who jumped on the other side of the street had done their best to fall feet down, but these fire-tortured, suffering ones fell inertly, as if they didn't care how they fell, just so that death came to them on the sidewalk instead of in the fiery furnace behind them.

The floods of water from the firemen's hose that ran in the gutter were actually stained red with blood.

On the sidewalk lay heaps of broken bodies. I saw a policeman later going about with tags, which he fastened with a wire to the wrists of the dead girls, numbering each of them with a lead pencil, and I saw him fasten tag No. 54 onto the wrist of a girl who wore an engagement ring.

A fireman who came downstairs from the building told me there were at least 50 bodies in the big room on the seventh floor. Another fireman told me that more girls had jumped down an air shaft in the rear of the building. I went back there, into the narrow court, and saw a heap of dead girls.

And there I saw the first fire escape I had seen. It was narrow. The fireman told me that many girls had gone down it and that others had fallen from it in the rush. But on the two fronts of the building there were no fire escapes.

These girls were all shirtwaist makers. As I looked at the heap of dead bodies I remembered their great strike of last year, in which these girls demanded more sanitary workrooms, and MORE SAFETY PRECAUTIONS in the shops. These dead bodies told the result.

Stop and Record

What do you think is the other side of this story? Make notes on your Critical Reading Chart (page 92).

Nonfiction

© GREAT SOURCE. ALL RIGHTS RESERVED.

Using the Strategy

Reading critically means reading the newspaper article slowly and carefully. Pay particular attention to key events the reporter describes. You can use an organizer to help you keep track of the chain of events.

• Use Sequence Notes to track the events a reporter describes.

Directions: Record the events of the Triangle Shirtwaist Factory fire in the order in which they occurred.

Sequence Notes

1. The building catches fire and workers rush to the windows for escape.

2.

3.

4.

5.

© GREAT SOURCE. ALL RIGHTS RESERVED.

NAME

FOR USE WITH PAGES 218-233

Understanding How Newspaper Articles Are Organized

Finding the facts in a newspaper article is easier if you understand how the information is organized. Many news stories follow a standard organization called a *funnel pattern.*

Directions: Show the organization of the Triangle Shirtwaist Factory fire article on this funnel.

Funnel Organizer

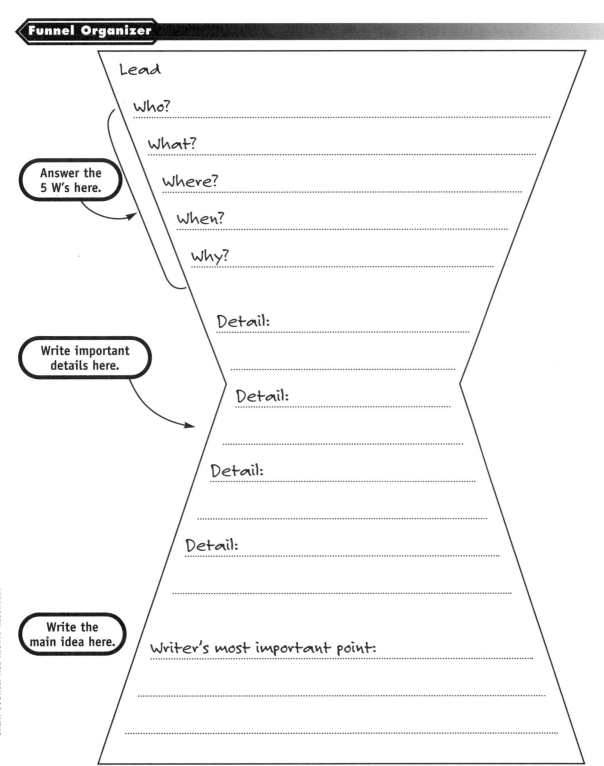

Answer the 5 W's here.

Lead

Who?

What?

Where?

When?

Why?

Write important details here.

Detail:

Detail:

Detail:

Detail:

Write the main idea here.

Writer's most important point:

Nonfiction

© GREAT SOURCE. ALL RIGHTS RESERVED.

E Connect

Making a connection to a newspaper article means reacting to what the reporter says.

• Record how the newspaper article made you feel.

The story about the Triangle Shirtwaist Factory fire made me feel

because

After Reading

After you've read a newspaper article, take the time to look back at what you've read.

F Pause and Reflect

At this point, consider whether you've met your reading purpose.

• Ask yourself some questions about the article you just finished.

Directions: Read each statement. Check *yes* or *no*.

Checklist	Yes	No
I can state the reporter's opinion in my own words.		
I can answer who, what, where, when, and why questions.		
I understand the reporter's evidence and have decided how reliable it is.		

© GREAT SOURCE. ALL RIGHTS RESERVED.

NAME FOR USE WITH PAGES 218-233

G Reread

If you're having trouble answering *yes* to the statements on the checklist, do some rereading.

• Use the strategy of summarizing when you reread.

Directions: Make Summary Notes about the article.

Summary Notes

Article headline:

Subject:

Author's viewpoint:

detail #1:

detail #2:

detail #3:

detail #4:

detail #5:

H Remember

Try to remember the most important details of an article so that you can talk about the subject later.

• Writing a brief summary can help you remember an article.

Directions: Write a brief summary of "Fire at a New York Shirtwaist Factory." Include only the most important details.

Summary

© GREAT SOURCE. ALL RIGHTS RESERVED.

Reading a Magazine Article

If your assignment is to read and respond to a magazine article, which tools and strategies should you use? How should you use them?

Before Reading

The strategy of questioning the author is an excellent one to use when you read a magazine article. Use this strategy and the reading process to help you understand and respond to an article about middle school stress.

A Set a Purpose

Before you turn to the article, establish a general purpose for reading. Ask yourself, "What do I hope to learn from the article?"

- **Use key words from the title of the article to form a reading purpose question.**

Directions: Write your purpose for reading the magazine article "Middle School Formula: High Stress = High Burnout."

My purpose:

B Preview

When you preview, look at the title, illustrations, headings, and first paragraph for clues about the topic of the article.

Directions: Preview the article and write your notes here.

My Preview Notes
The title of the article:
I learned this from the first paragraph:
I learned this from the illustrations:
I learned this from the headings:

© GREAT SOURCE. ALL RIGHTS RESERVED.

NAME

FOR USE WITH PAGES 234-246

MIDDLE SCHOOL FORMULA:

HIGH STRESS = High Burnout

Rosaline Silvi attends George Washington Middle School in suburban New York. Silvi's school is probably typical of most middle schools around the country. It's a little on the crowded side, a little on the underfunded side, and maybe a little on the run-down side. Rosaline's middle school is typical in one other way, as well. It is filled to capacity and then some with students who are stressed to the maximum. Rosaline and her peers are frantically worried about grades, test scores, and national rankings. They're also worried about which extracurricular activities will look best on their school records and whether or not they have what it takes to cut it in high school and beyond.

In decades past, the middle school years were quiet ones. Teachers viewed this time as an opportunity for students to mature physically, socially, and academically at their own pace. In fact, middle school was regarded as a sort of low-tension bridge between the easygoing elementary years and the academically charged high school years.

Nonfiction

© GREAT SOURCE. ALL RIGHTS RESERVED.

In recent years, however, life in middle school has changed dramatically. Gone is the slow and easy pace and the emphasis on the "whole child." In fact, many of today's middle schools are as highly charged and achievement-oriented as the private high school around the corner.

"There's this constant pressure to succeed in my school," explains Silvi. "I couldn't believe how hard things got the minute I moved up to middle school. The tests are harder, the books are harder, the sports are harder—everything is harder."

Stop and Record

What is the topic of this article? Write your answer on page 104.

The "New" Middle School

Most teachers, principals, and students would probably agree with Silvi's complaint, but no one seems to know what to do about it. "It's not that we don't know what the problem is," explains John Gross, principal of Rockridge Middle School in southern North Carolina. "Students, parents, and teachers now think of middle school as a testing ground for high school performance and that causes a great deal of anxiety. Middle school teachers of today feel compelled to push students harder in the hopes that this will better prepare them for the competitive atmosphere that is a part of most high schools," he says. The result is "middle schools that offer plenty of academic opportunities but few opportunities for social or emotional growth."

The result is "middle schools that offer plenty of academic opportunities but few opportunities for social or emotional growth."

Most educators agree that the years between the fifth and ninth grades are important ones—as important, in fact, as the preschool years. Yet very little research has been done to explore what happens when the pressure is turned up too high in middle school. "It's a scary trend right now," explains Dr. Janet Garvey, school psychologist. "I'm seeing seventh and eighth graders who are totally overwhelmed by school and extracurricular activities. They are pushed to do more and more and more, and some simply can't keep up. What I fear is that these high-stressed middle schoolers will be totally burned out before they get anywhere near the high school."

Stop and Record

What point is the author making about today's middle schools? Write your answer on page 104.

© GREAT SOURCE. ALL RIGHTS RESERVED.

NAME

"Middle School Formula: High Stress = High Burnout," continued

Making Changes for the Better

So what's a middle school student—or parent of a middle school student—to do? Garvey and other school psychologists suggest that the first step in fighting middle school stress is to turn down teacher and parental expectations for students. "I don't want to hear a sixth grader talking about getting into a good college," Garvey says. "Sixth grade is simply *too early* to be worrying about college. Instead, they should be focusing on getting to know themselves and their peers."

Principal Gross agrees. He takes Garvey's suggestion one step further. "Helping students relax is an important part of a teacher's job," he explains. Middle school teachers need to slow down a bit, he says, and give students a chance to digest what they've learned. "Otherwise," he warns, "you end up with ninth graders who are crammed full of facts, but who are just sick to death of learning. That's simply not right."

Nonfiction

Stop and Record

What does the author say we can do to fix the problems in today's middle schools? Write your answer on page 104.

C Plan

After your preview, make a reading plan. What strategy can help you find and understand the topic, main idea, and supporting details of this article?

- **Use the strategy of questioning the author to help you get *more* from a magazine article.**

Questioning the author involves thinking about the decisions the author made. It can help you spot the writer's main idea and see how it is supported.

© GREAT SOURCE. ALL RIGHTS RESERVED.

During Reading

Now go back and do a careful reading of "Middle School Formula: High Stress = High Burnout." Stop along the way to ask some questions of the author. Write your answers below.

D Read with a Purpose

Keep in mind your purpose for reading. Remember that you're looking for information about the subject, main idea, and supporting details.

Directions: Write answers to your questions here.

What is the subject of the article?

What point is the author making about today's middle schools?

What does the author say we can do to fix the problems in today's middle schools?

Using the Strategy

Remember that one of the reasons you're questioning the author is to find out the main idea of the article. A graphic organizer like the one on the next page can help you keep track of your thoughts.

- **Use a Main Idea Organizer to keep track of important information in a magazine article.**

© GREAT SOURCE. ALL RIGHTS RESERVED.

NAME

FOR USE WITH PAGES 234-246

Main Idea Organizer

Subject: Middle school stress		
Author's viewpoint:		
Detail #1:	**Detail #2:**	**Detail #3:**

Nonfiction

Understanding How Magazine Articles Are Organized

Like news stories, magazine articles must answer the five questions: *who, what, where, when,* and *why*. Looking for answers to the five W's can strengthen your understanding of the writer's main idea.

Directions: Complete this 5 W's Organizer with information from "Middle School Formula: High Stress = High Burnout."

5 W's Organizer

Subject

Note the subject here.

Who

Where

Why

What

When

© GREAT SOURCE. ALL RIGHTS RESERVED.

E Connect

It's important to react to what you learn in a magazine article.

- **Recording your reactions can help you process and remember what you've learned.**

Directions: In the first sentence, circle *agree* or *disagree*. Then complete these statements.

I agree / disagree that middle school stress is a problem. Here's why:

In my school, kids feel stressed about and

Here's what teachers and students can do to solve the problem:

After Reading

Now that you've finished the article, your job is to decide whether or not you agree with the author's main idea.

F Pause and Reflect

Begin by reflecting on your purpose.

- **To reflect on your purpose, ask yourself, "Have I accomplished what I set out to do?"**

Directions: Check *yes* or *no* to the items on this list.

Checklist	Yes	No
I have learned several important facts about middle school stress.		
I know what the author's main idea is.		
I agree with the author's main idea.		

© GREAT SOURCE. ALL RIGHTS RESERVED.

NAME

FOR USE WITH PAGES 234-246

G Reread

As a critical reader, you must weigh the evidence for and against a magazine writer's viewpoint.

- **Use the strategy of reading critically to evaluate the viewpoint and evidence presented.**

Directions: Read the viewpoint and evidence on this Argument Chart. Then write your opinion of it.

Argument Chart

Viewpoint: Middle school students are under too much stress.

Supporting Evidence	Is it sound? Is it persuasive?
Rosaline Silvi's story	
Facts and details about today's middle schoolers	
Principal Gross's comments	
Dr. Garvey's comments	

© GREAT SOURCE. ALL RIGHTS RESERVED.

NAME

H Remember

Take what you've learned from a magazine article and apply it to your own life. This can help you remember what you've read.

- **To remember a magazine article, connect what you've read to your own life.**

Directions: Make a list of five things you can do to avoid burnout in your years in middle school. Explain your ideas.

My Ideas	Explanation
1.	
2.	
3.	
4.	
5.	

© GREAT SOURCE. ALL RIGHTS RESERVED.

NAME FOR USE WITH PAGES 247-255

Focus on Persuasive Writing

Persuasive writing makes an argument. Your job as reader is to understand and evaluate the argument the writer presents. This three-step plan can help.

Step 1: Find the topic and viewpoint.

The **topic** is what the article or essay is about. The **viewpoint** is the author's main point or opinion about the topic.

Directions: Read the first two paragraphs of this editorial. Circle the topic. Highlight the viewpoint.

Zoo Fire: A Community Disgrace

The fire started small. At first, there was only a little smoke and just a flame or two. It could have been put out in a minute by a quick-thinking zookeeper. Unfortunately, no one was watching. The little fire grew into a great, big fire that spread up and down the halls of the lion house and crept under the bars of every cage. Almost before anyone knew it had started, six lions were dead and five tigers were badly burned.

The fire at the zoo was caused by a frayed wire. It could have happened anywhere. Yet it happened at *our* zoo, to *our* animals, and that makes it *our* problem. Six animals died under our watch. This means that every single man, woman, and child who visited the zoo since it opened twenty years ago was responsible for the death of these animals.

Step 2: Locate the writer's support for the viewpoint.

Good persuasive writers know they must support their viewpoint with convincing facts and details.

Directions: Read the rest of the editorial. Underline three details that support the viewpoint.

© GREAT SOURCE. ALL RIGHTS RESERVED.

"Zoo Fire: A Community Disgrace," continued

But how could I be responsible, you ask? You're responsible because you—and every other person in this city—said nothing when you saw those big, beautiful animals living in those cramped cages. How could we have let our lions and tigers spend day after day pacing the four walls while we stood outside the safety bars? Why didn't anyone object? Why didn't we say to the zoo, "Listen, you need a better environment for your lions and tigers. They need a big outdoor space with trees for climbing and water for bathing." Other zoos have these kinds of natural environments for their animals. Why didn't we?

It's too late now for us to do anything about the dead lions. But we can do something to help the big cats who did survive the fire—and maybe some of the other animals at the zoo as well.

Here's what we can do. We can write letters to the zoo. We can insist that they get rid of the cages and create a habitat for these animals. We can offer our money and our help. If we have to, we can stay away from the zoo until they promise to get rid of the cages. Then we'll come back again and show the zoo management that we're willing to help.

Step 3: Evaluate the argument.

After you finish reading, decide how you feel about the writer's argument.

Directions: Complete the Argument Chart on the next page. Write the viewpoint you highlighted and the evidence you underlined. Then say how the argument applies to your life and how it makes you feel.

© GREAT SOURCE. ALL RIGHTS RESERVED.

NAME

FOR USE WITH PAGES 247-255

Argument Chart

Viewpoint	Support	My Opinion
	#1	
	#2	
	#3	
Write the author's viewpoint here.	List the support the writer gives here.	Write your response to the argument here.

Nonfiction

© GREAT SOURCE. ALL RIGHTS RESERVED.

Focus on Speeches

Using the reading process when you read a speech can help you understand and evaluate the speaker's message.

Step 1: Find the speaker's purpose.

As you read, look for clues about the speaker's purpose. Ask yourself *who, what, where, when,* and *why* questions about the speech.

Directions: Read the background information and speech that follow. Then complete the 5 W's Organizer.

from "My Heart Feels Like Bursting" by Satanta, 1867

Satanta (1830–1878) was second chief of the Kiowa Indian Nation during the mid-1800s. In 1867, he and other Plains Indians chiefs were forced to sign a treaty that restricted where the Plains tribes could live and hunt. In this speech, delivered at Medicine Lodge Creek, Kansas, Satanta explains his feelings about the treaty and how his people have been treated.

I love the land and the buffalo and will not part with it. I want you to understand well what I say. . . . I have heard that you intend to settle us on a reservation near the mountains. I don't want to settle. I love to roam over the prairies. There I feel free and happy, but when we settle down, we grow pale and die. I have laid aside my lance, bow, and shield, and yet I feel safe in your presence. I have told you the truth. I have no little lies hidden about me, but I don't know how it is with the commissioners. Are they as clear as I am? A long time ago this land belonged to our fathers; but when I go up to the river, I see camps of soldiers on its banks. The soldiers cut down my timber; they kill my buffalo; and when I see that, my heart feels like bursting; I feel sorry. I have spoken.

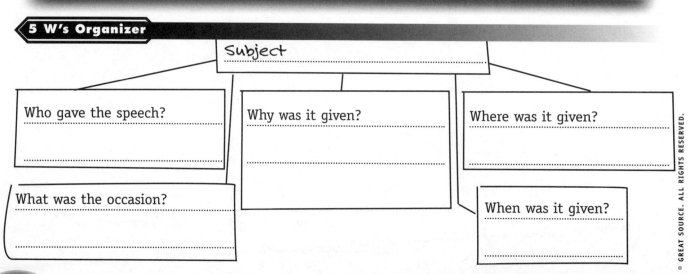

5 W's Organizer

Subject

Who gave the speech?

Why was it given?

Where was it given?

What was the occasion?

When was it given?

© GREAT SOURCE. ALL RIGHTS RESERVED.

NAME

FOR USE WITH PAGES 256-264

Step 2: Identify the viewpoint.

To find the speaker's viewpoint, look for the subject of the speech and what the speaker says about it.

Topic of the speech	+	What Satanta says	=	His viewpoint
The Medicine Lodge Treaty	+		=	

Step 3: Find support for the viewpoint.

For a viewpoint to be convincing, the speaker must support it with strong evidence.

Directions: Complete this organizer. Use details from Satanta's speech.

Viewpoint:

Supporting Evidence

Facts:	Personal Experience:	Personal Experience:

© GREAT SOURCE. ALL RIGHTS RESERVED.

Focus on Real-world Writing

Real-world, or informational, writing helps you stay informed about the world around you. Follow these steps when reading this type of writing.

Step 1: Identify your purpose.

First, know your purpose for reading.

Directions: Look at this flier for a school event. What is your purpose for reading?

My purpose is ....

....

All Students of Dorothea Dix Middle School!!!

It's time for our annual holiday dance!!!!

Date: Friday, December 1

Time: 7:00 P.M. to 10:00 P.M.

Dress: Casual

Sponsor: Dorothea Dix Middle School PTO

Don't miss out on the best school dance of the year! Our very own dance band, the DDMS Players, will be on stage for the entire evening!

Come in pairs or with a group!

Refreshments! Photos! Games! Contests! Prizes!

Rules: Students must dress appropriately. No T-shirts or sandals. Doors will open at 7:00 P.M. No student will be admitted after 7:30. All guests must present a DDMS ID card to enter the dance. Students caught breaking a school rule will be given a Level III detention.

© GREAT SOURCE. ALL RIGHTS RESERVED.

NAME ______________________ FOR USE WITH PAGES 265-272

Step 2: Understand the organization.

For real-world reading, you want to see how the writing is organized—and fast.

Directions: Look for words in large or boldface type and for headings. Then use the information to complete this Web.

Web

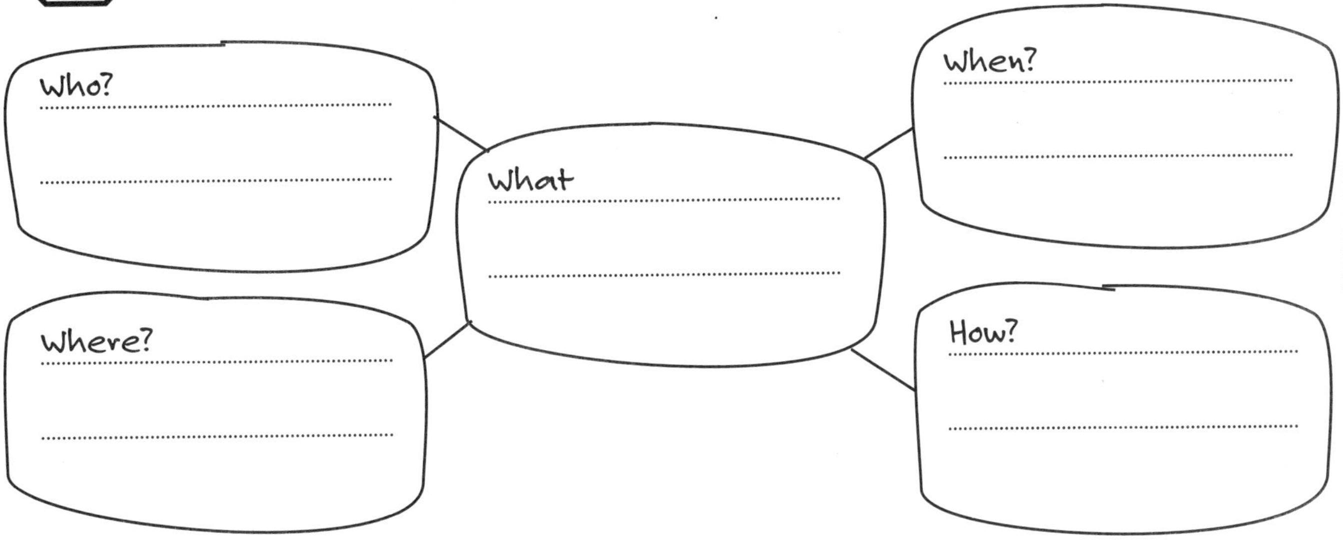

Step 3: Apply the information to your own life.

Figure out a way to remember key information from the writing. Also decide how it affects you personally.

Directions: Write information about the school dance on this calendar page. Include only what's important to you personally.

Nonfiction

© GREAT SOURCE. ALL RIGHTS RESERVED.

Reading a Short Story

Everybody loves a good story, but some stories are more challenging than others. What can you do to make challenging stories easier and more fun to read? Try asking yourself questions and finding the answers.

Before Reading

Get ready to ask and answer questions. Use the reading process and the strategy of using graphic organizers to read and respond to a famous story by the French writer Guy de Maupassant. You may already know this story. Here's your chance to know it in a new way.

A Set a Purpose

Your purpose is your reason for reading. Setting your purpose first, before you begin reading, can help you get *more* from a story.

• To set your purpose, turn the title of the story into a question.

Directions: Write your purpose for reading Maupassant's "The Diamond Necklace" below. Then predict what you think the story will be about.

My purpose: ....

....

My prediction: ....

....

....

....

....

....

....

....

© GREAT SOURCE. ALL RIGHTS RESERVED.

NAME

FOR USE WITH PAGES 294–314

B Preview

Preview a short story before you begin reading. Skim the background section first. Then take a peek at the first few paragraphs. Highlight words and phrases you think are important, interesting, or puzzling.

Directions: Write your notes in this chart.

Preview Questions	My Notes
What is the title of the story?	
Who is the author?	
What did you learn from the background?	
What ideas did the first two paragraphs give you about the story?	
What repeated words did you see?	

Fiction

© GREAT SOURCE. ALL RIGHTS RESERVED.

The Diamond Necklace

by

Guy de Maupassant

What you need to know . . .

THE SELECTION "The Diamond Necklace" is one of Guy de Maupassant's most famous short stories. In this work, Maupassant explores the theme of misfortune and shows how even a small mistake can lead to terrible ruin. This is an idea that Maupassant returned to again and again in his writing.

THE AUTHOR Guy de Maupassant (1850–1893) is said to be the greatest French short story writer of all time. He wrote more than three hundred stories. Through them, he offers a fascinating glimpse of French life from 1870 to 1890.

THE THEME Misfortune

LITERARY FOCUS Characterization

FURTHER READING "Alexandre" and "The Trip of Le Horla" by Guy de Maupassant

© GREAT SOURCE. ALL RIGHTS RESERVED.

NAME FOR USE WITH PAGES 294–314

"The Diamond Necklace" by Guy de Maupassant

The girl was one of those pretty and charming young creatures who sometimes are born, as if by a slip of fate, into a family of clerks. She had no dowry, no expectations, no way of being known, understood, loved, married by any rich and distinguished man; so she let herself be married to a little clerk of the Ministry of Public Instruction.

She dressed plainly because she could not dress well, but she was unhappy as if she had really fallen from a higher station; since with women there is neither caste nor rank, for beauty, grace and charm take the place of family and birth. Natural ingenuity, instinct for what is elegant, a supple mind are their sole hierarchy, and often make of women of the people the equals of the very greatest ladies.

Mathilde suffered ceaselessly, feeling herself born to enjoy all delicacies and all luxuries. She was distressed at the poverty of her dwelling, at the bareness of the walls, at the shabby chairs, the ugliness of the curtains. All those things, of which another woman of her rank would never even have been conscious, tortured her and made her angry. The sight of the little Breton peasant who did her humble housework aroused in her despairing regrets and bewildering dreams. She thought of silent antechambers hung with Oriental tapestry, illumined by tall bronze candelabra, and of two great footmen in knee breeches who sleep in the big armchairs, made drowsy by the oppressive heat of the stove. She thought of long reception halls hung with ancient silk, of the dainty cabinets containing priceless curiosities and of the little coquettish perfumed reception rooms made for chatting at five o'clock with intimate friends, with men famous and sought after, whom all women envy and whose attention they all desire.

When she sat down to dinner, before the round table covered with a tablecloth in use three days, opposite her husband, who uncovered the soup tureen and declared with a delighted air, "Ah, the good soup! I don't know anything better than that," she thought of dainty dinners, of shining silverware, of tapestry that peopled the walls with ancient personages and with strange birds flying in the midst of a fairy forest; and she thought of delicious dishes served on marvellous plates and of the whispered gallantries to which you listen with a sphinxlike smile while you are eating the pink meat of a trout or the wings of a quail.

She had no gowns, no jewels, nothing. And she loved nothing but that. She felt made for that. She would have liked so much to please, to be envied, to be charming, to be sought after.

She had a friend, a former schoolmate at the convent, who was rich, and whom she did not like to go to see any more because she felt so sad when she came home.

But one evening her husband reached home with a triumphant air and holding a large envelope in his hand.

"There," said he, "there is something for you."

Fiction

© GREAT SOURCE. ALL RIGHTS RESERVED.

She tore the paper quickly and drew out a printed card which bore these words:

The Minister of Public Instruction and Madame Georges Ramponneau request the honor of M. and Madame Loisel's company at the palace of the Ministry on Monday evening, January 18th.

Stop and Record:

Make some notes in the "Beginning" section of the Story Organizer (page 126).

Instead of being delighted, as her husband had hoped, she threw the invitation on the table crossly, muttering:

"What do you wish me to do with that?"

"Why, my dear, I thought you would be glad. You never go out, and this is such a fine opportunity. I had great trouble to get it. Every one wants to go; it is very select, and they are not giving many invitations to clerks. The whole official world will be there."

She looked at him with an irritated glance and said impatiently:

"And what do you wish me to put on my back?"

He had not thought of that. He stammered:

"Why, the gown you go to the theatre in. It looks very well to me."

He stopped, distracted, seeing that his wife was weeping. Two great tears ran slowly from the corners of her eyes toward the corners of her mouth.

"What's the matter? What's the matter?" he answered.

By a violent effort she conquered her grief and replied in a calm voice, while she wiped her wet cheeks:

"Nothing. Only I have no gown, and, therefore, I can't go to this ball. Give your card to some colleague whose wife is better equipped than I am."

He was in despair. He resumed:

"Come, let us see, Mathilde. How much would it cost, a suitable gown, which you could use on other occasions—something very simple?"

She reflected several seconds, making her calculations and wondering also what sum she could ask without drawing on herself an immediate refusal and a frightened exclamation from the economical clerk.

Finally she replied hesitating:

"I don't know exactly, but I think I could manage it with four hundred francs."

He grew a little pale, because he was laying aside just that amount to buy a gun and treat himself to a little shooting next summer on the plain of Nanterre, with several friends who went to shoot larks there of a Sunday.

© GREAT SOURCE. ALL RIGHTS RESERVED.

NAME

"The Diamond Necklace" by Guy de Maupassant, continued

But he said:

"Very well. I will give you four hundred francs. And try to have a pretty gown."

The day of the ball drew near and Madame Loisel seemed sad, uneasy, anxious. Her frock was ready, however. Her husband said to her one evening:

"What is the matter? Come, you have seemed very strange these last three days."

And she answered:

"It annoys me not to have a single piece of jewelry, not a single ornament, nothing to put on. I shall look poverty-stricken. I would almost rather not go at all."

"You might wear natural flowers," said her husband. "They're very stylish at this time of year. For ten francs you can get two or three magnificent roses."

She was not convinced.

"No; there's nothing more humiliating than to look poor among other women who are rich."

"How stupid you are!" her husband cried. "Go look up your friend, Madame Forestier, and ask her to lend you some jewels. You're intimate enough with her to do that."

She uttered a cry of joy:

"True! I never thought of it."

The next day she went to her friend and told her of her distress.

Madame Forestier went to a wardrobe with a mirror, took out a large jewel box, brought it back, opened it and said to Madame Loisel:

"Choose, my dear."

She saw first some bracelets, then a pearl necklace, then a Venetian gold cross set with precious stones, of admirable workmanship. She tried on the ornaments before the mirror, hesitated and could not make up her mind to part with them, to give them back. She kept asking:

"Haven't you any more?"

"Why, yes. Look further; I don't know what you like."

Suddenly she discovered, in a black satin box, a superb diamond necklace, and her heart throbbed with an immoderate desire. Her hands trembled as she took it. She fastened it round her throat, outside her high-necked waist, and was lost in ecstasy at her reflection in the mirror.

Then she asked, hesitating, filled with anxious doubt:

"Will you lend me this, only this?"

"Why, yes, certainly."

She threw her arms round her friend's neck, then fled with her treasure.

The night of the ball arrived. Madame Loisel was a great success. She was prettier than any other woman present, elegant, graceful, smiling and wild with joy. All the men looked at her, asked her name, sought to be introduced. All the attaches of the Cabinet wished to waltz with her. She was remarked by the minister himself.

© GREAT SOURCE. ALL RIGHTS RESERVED.

She danced with rapture, with passion, intoxicated by pleasure, forgetting all in the triumph of her beauty, in the glory of her success, in a sort of cloud of happiness comprised of all this homage, admiration, these awakened desires and of that sense of triumph which is so sweet to woman's heart.

She left the ball about four o'clock in the morning. Her husband had been sleeping since midnight in a little deserted anteroom with three other gentlemen whose wives were enjoying the ball.

He threw over her shoulders the wraps he had brought, the modest wraps of common life, the poverty of which contrasted with the elegance of the ball dress. She felt this and wished to escape so as not to be remarked by the other women, who were enveloping themselves in costly furs.

Loisel held her back, saying: "Wait a bit. You will catch cold outside. I will call a cab."

But she did not listen to him and rapidly descended the stairs. When they reached the street they could not find a carriage and began to look for one, shouting after the cabmen passing at a distance.

They went toward the Seine in despair, shivering with cold. At last they found on the quay one of those ancient night cabs which, as though they were ashamed to show their shabbiness during the day, are never seen round Paris until after dark.

It took them to their dwelling in the Rue des Martyrs, and sadly they mounted the stairs to their flat. All was ended for her. As to him, he reflected that he must be at the ministry at ten o'clock that morning.

She removed her wraps before the glass so as to see herself once more in all her glory. But suddenly she uttered a cry. She no longer had the necklace around her neck!

"What is the matter with you?" demanded her husband, already half undressed.

She turned distractedly toward him.

"I have—I have—I've lost Madame Forestier's necklace," she cried.

He stood up, bewildered.

"What!—how? Impossible!"

They looked among the folds of her skirt, of her cloak, in her pockets, everywhere, but did not find it.

"You're sure you had it on when you left the ball?" he asked.

"Yes, I felt it in the vestibule of the minister's house."

"But if you had lost it in the street we should have heard it fall. It must be in the cab."

"Yes, probably. Did you take his number?"

"No. And you—didn't you notice it?"

"No."

They looked, thunderstruck, at each other. At last Loisel put on his clothes.

"I shall go back on foot," said he, "over the whole route, to see whether I can find it."

He went out. She sat waiting on a chair in her ball dress, without strength to go to

© GREAT SOURCE. ALL RIGHTS RESERVED.

NAME

FOR USE WITH PAGES 294–314

"The Diamond Necklace" by Guy de Maupassant, continued

bed, overwhelmed, without any fire, without a thought.

Her husband returned about seven o'clock. He had found nothing.

He went to police headquarters, to the newspaper offices to offer a reward; he went to the cab companies—everywhere, in fact, whither he was urged by the least spark of hope.

She waited all day, in the same condition of mad fear before this terrible calamity.

Loisel returned at night with a hollow, pale face. He had discovered nothing.

"You must write to your friend," said he, "that you have broken the clasp of her necklace and that you are having it mended. That will give us time to turn round."

She wrote at his dictation.

Stop and Record

Make some notes in the "Middle" section of the Story Organizer (page 126).

At the end of a week they had lost all hope. Loisel, who had aged five years, declared:

"We must consider how to replace that ornament."

The next day they took the box that had contained it and went to the jeweler whose name was found within. He consulted his books.

"It was not I, madame, who sold that necklace; I must simply have furnished the case."

Then they went from jeweler to jeweler, searching for a necklace like the other, trying to recall it, both sick with chagrin and grief.

They found, in a shop at the Palais Royal, a string of diamonds that seemed to them exactly like the one they had lost. It was worth forty thousand francs. They could have it for thirty-six.

So they begged the jeweler not to sell it for three days yet. And they made a bargain that he should buy it back for thirty-four thousand francs, in case they should find the lost necklace before the end of February.

Loisel possessed eighteen thousand francs which his father had left him. He would borrow the rest.

He did borrow, asking a thousand francs of one, five hundred of another, five louis here, three louis there. He gave notes, took up ruinous obligations, dealt with usurers and all the race of lenders. He compromised all the rest of his life, risked signing a note without even knowing whether he could meet it; and, frightened by the trouble yet to come, by the black misery that was about to fall upon him, by the prospect of all the physical privations and moral tortures that he was to suffer, he went to get the new necklace, laying upon the jeweler's counter thirty-six thousand francs.

© GREAT SOURCE. ALL RIGHTS RESERVED.

When Madame Loisel took back the necklace Madame Forestier said to her with a chilly manner:

"You should have returned it sooner; I might have needed it."

She did not open the case, as her friend had so much feared. If she had detected the substitution, what would she have thought, what would she have said? Would she not have taken Madame Loisel for a thief?

Thereafter Madame Loisel knew the horrible existence of the needy. She bore her part, however, with sudden heroism. That dreadful debt must be paid. She would pay it. They dismissed their servant; they changed their lodgings; they rented a garret under the roof.

She came to know what heavy housework meant and the odious cares of the kitchen. She washed the dishes, using her dainty fingers and rosy nails on greasy pots and pans. She washed the soiled linen, the shirts and the dishcloths, which she dried upon a line; she carried the slops down to the street every morning and carried up the water, stopping for breath at every landing. And dressed like a woman of the people, she went to the fruiterer, the grocer, the butcher, a basket on her arm, bargaining, meeting with impertinence, defending her miserable money, sou by sou.

Every month they had to meet some notes, renew others, obtain more time.

Her husband worked evenings, making up a tradesman's accounts, and late at night he often copied manuscript for five sous a page.

This life lasted ten years.

At the end of ten years they had paid everything, everything, with the rates of usury and the accumulations of the compound interest.

Madame Loisel looked old now. She had become the woman of impoverished households—strong and hard and rough. With frowsy hair, skirts askew and red hands, she talked loud while washing the floor with great swishes of water. But sometimes, when her husband was at the office, she sat down near the window and she thought of that evening of long ago, of that ball where she had been so beautiful and so admired.

What would have happened if she had not lost that necklace? Who knows? who knows? How strange and changeful is life! How small a thing is needed to make or ruin us!

But one Sunday, having gone to take a walk in the Champs Elysees to refresh herself after the labors of the week, she suddenly perceived a woman who was leading a child. It was Madame Forestier, still young, still beautiful, still charming.

Madame Loisel felt moved. Should she speak to her? Yes, certainly. And now that she had paid, she would tell her all about it. Why not?

She went up.

"Good-day, Jeanne."

© GREAT SOURCE. ALL RIGHTS RESERVED.

NAME

"The Diamond Necklace" by Guy de Maupassant, continued

The other, astonished to be familiarly addressed by this plain good-wife, did not recognize her at all and stammered:

"But—madame!—I do not know—— You must have mistaken.

"No. I am Mathilde Loisel."

Her friend uttered a cry.

"Oh, my poor Mathilde! How you are changed!"

"Yes, I have had a pretty hard life, since I last saw you, and great poverty—and that because of you!"

"Of me! How so?"

"Do you remember that diamond necklace you lent me to wear at the ministerial ball?"

"Yes. Well?"

"Well, I lost it."

"What do you mean? You brought it back."

"I brought you back another exactly like it. And it has taken us ten years to pay for it. You can understand that it was not easy for us, for us who had nothing. At last it is ended, and I am very glad."

Madame Forestier had stopped.

"You say that you bought a necklace of diamonds to replace mine?"

"Yes. You never noticed it, then! They were very similar."

And she smiled with a joy that was at once proud and ingenuous.

Madame Forestier, deeply moved, took her hands.

"Oh, my poor Mathilde! Why, my necklace was paste! It was worth at most only five hundred francs!"

Stop and Record

Make some notes in the "End" section of the Story Organizer (page 126).

C Plan

Next make a plan. How can you best meet your reading purpose? A graphic organizer can help.

- **Practice the strategy of using graphic organizers.**

A Story Organizer can help you keep track of the events of the plot.

© GREAT SOURCE. ALL RIGHTS RESERVED.

During Reading

D Read with a Purpose

Directions: Now go back and do a careful reading of Maupassant's story. As you read, make notes on this organizer.

Story Organizer

Beginning	Middle	End

Using the Strategy

Many kinds of graphic organizers work well with short stories.

• Use an Inference Chart to gather your ideas about a character.

Directions: Record information about Madame Loisel in the Inference Chart.

Inference Chart

What Madame Loisel says or does	What I can conclude

© GREAT SOURCE. ALL RIGHTS RESERVED.

NAME .... FOR USE WITH PAGES 294–314

Understanding How Stories Are Organized

Short stories generally follow a pattern. You can map the organization of a story with a graphic similar to the one on page 309 of your handbook.

Directions: Use this Plot Diagram to show the organization of "The Diamond Necklace." Include the important details.

Plot Diagram

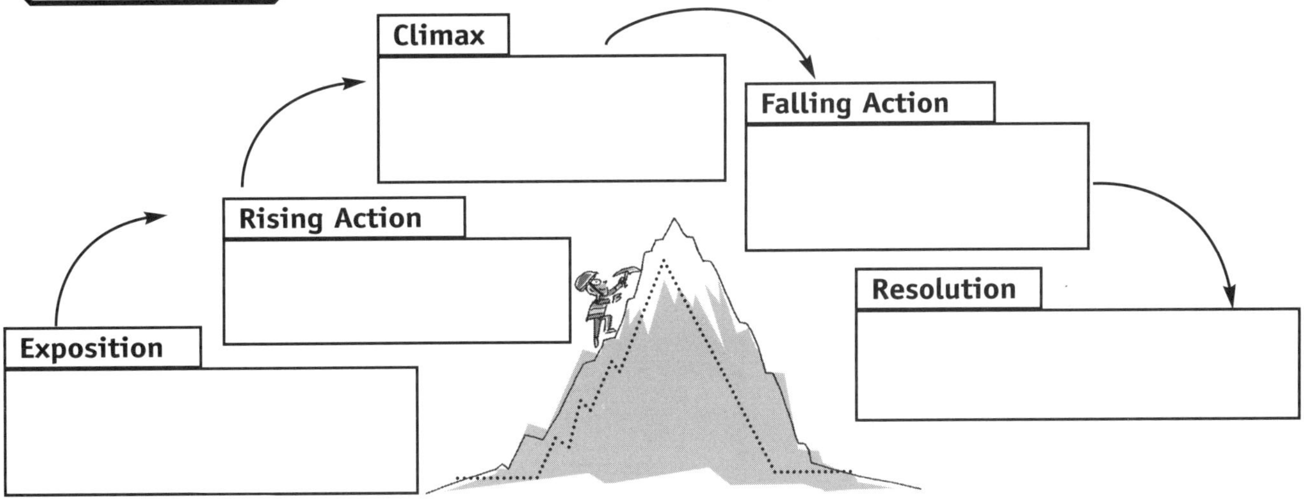

E Connect

"The Diamond Necklace" has a surprise ending. How did it make you feel?

• **Record how the ending of the story made you feel.**

Directions: Write your response to the ending on the line below.

The ending made me feel ....

After Reading

After reading most stories, you will have questions. This is because good writing makes you think about possibilities and ideas. Follow up by going back through the story again and looking for answers to your questions.

F Pause and Reflect

The surprise ending of "The Diamond Necklace" forces you to go back and look at the story again. How well did you meet your reading purpose?

Thoughts about my purpose: ....

....

Fiction

© GREAT SOURCE. ALL RIGHTS RESERVED.

G Reread

You can sharpen your understanding of a story if you reread important parts using the strategy of close reading. When you do a close reading, you read small bits of the story very carefully, word for word.

• A powerful rereading strategy to use is close reading.

Directions: Look at the lines from "The Diamond Necklace" in the first column. Write your response to the lines in the second column.

Double-entry Journal

Text of "The Diamond Necklace"	My Response
"Mathilde suffered ceaselessly, feeling herself born to enjoy all delicacies and all luxuries."	
"What would have happened if she had not lost that necklace?. . . How small a thing is needed to make or ruin us!"	
"'Oh, my poor Mathilde! Why my necklace was paste! It was worth at most only five hundred francs!'"	

H Remember

Good readers remember what they've read.

• To remember a story, make the information in the story your own.

On another sheet of paper, write a journal entry about "The Diamond Necklace." Say what you did and didn't like about the story, and support your viewpoint with details. Be sure to discuss the surprise ending.

© GREAT SOURCE. ALL RIGHTS RESERVED.

NAME FOR USE WITH PAGES 315–339

Reading a Novel

Reading a novel is like going on an adventure. You should enjoy the journey. You'll discover some interesting people, places, and ideas. The key is to stay focused and pay attention to what happens.

Before Reading

Some novels are long and complex. There's a lot going on at once. How can you figure out what's really important? One way is to use the strategy of synthesizing. Begin by setting your purpose.

Fiction

A Set a Purpose

Think of your purpose as a way to look at six elements of the novel: point of view, characters, setting, plot, theme, and style.

• Ask important questions about the major elements of the novel.

Directions: You will be reading Chapter 1 of *The Secret Garden,* "There Is No One Left." What will be your purpose for reading? Write your questions about the six major elements below. (We've done the first one for you.)

Purpose Chart

Element	My Question
Point of view	Who is telling the story?
Characters	
Setting	
Plot	
Theme	
Style	

© GREAT SOURCE. ALL RIGHTS RESERVED.

B Preview

Always preview a novel before you read it. Begin by looking at the front and back covers. What information can you find?

Directions: Preview *The Secret Garden*. Write important information on the sticky notes.

1. The title is:

2. The author is:

Back Cover

Take a tour of Frances Hodgson Burnett's unforgettable secret garden. . . .

Frances Hodgson Burnett was born in northern England in 1849. Burnett began writing when she was a teenager. Her novels and stories met with immediate success. Her most beloved book, *The Secret Garden,* tells the story of Mary Lennox, a spoiled, sickly child who is sent to live with her uncle after her parents die in an epidemic. She is fascinated by a locked garden outside her uncle's house. The garden Burnett describes in the novel is similar to a rose garden that she knew and loved.

3. Important information about the author:

Front Cover

Classics Books Presents. . .

The Secret Garden

BY Frances Hodgson Burnett

4. Important information about the book:

© GREAT SOURCE. ALL RIGHTS RESERVED.

NAME ______ FOR USE WITH PAGES 315–339

C Plan

How can you keep track of all six elements as you read? The strategy of synthesizing can help. When you synthesize, you look at a number of parts or elements separately and then pull them together to see how they work with each other.

- **Use the strategy of synthesizing to understand the major elements and see how they work together in the novel.**

During Reading

D Read with a Purpose

Focus on three of the elements as you read Chapter 1 of *The Secret Garden.*

Directions: Read Chapter 1 from *The Secret Garden.* Make notes about the elements of setting, characters, and plot on your Fiction Organizer. You'll come back to the theme element later.

Fiction

Fiction Organizer

The Secret Garden

Setting Where and when does the chapter take place?

______

Characters Who are they? What are they like?

______

Plot What happens?

______

Theme What is the author's message?

______

© GREAT SOURCE. ALL RIGHTS RESERVED.

from *The Secret Garden* by Frances Hodgson Burnett

Chapter 1 There Is No One Left

When Mary Lennox was sent to Misselthwaite Manor to live with her uncle everybody said she was the most disagreeable-looking child ever seen. It was true, too. She had a little thin face and a little thin body, thin light hair and a sour expression. Her hair was yellow, and her face was yellow because she had been born in India and had always been ill in one way or another. Her father had held a position under the English Government and had always been busy and ill himself, and her mother had been a great beauty who cared only to go to parties and amuse herself with gay people. She had not wanted a little girl at all, and when Mary was born she handed her over to the care of an Ayah, who was made to understand that if she wished to please the Mem Sahib she must keep the child out of sight as much as possible. So when she was a sickly, fretful, ugly little baby she was kept out of the way, and when she became a sickly, fretful, toddling thing she was kept out of the way also. She never remembered seeing familiarly anything but the dark faces of her Ayah and the other native servants, and as they always obeyed her and gave her her own way in everything, because the Mem Sahib would be angry if she was disturbed by her crying, by the time she was six years old she was as tyrannical and selfish a little pig as ever lived. The young English governess who came to teach her to read and write disliked her so much that she gave up her place in three months, and when other governesses came to try to fill it they always went away in a shorter time than the first one. So if Mary had not chosen to really want to know how to read books she would never have learned her letters at all.

Stop and Record

Make some notes in the "Setting" section of the Fiction Organizer (page 131). In what country was Mary born? Where is she being sent?

One frightfully hot morning, when she was about nine years old, she awakened feeling very cross, and she became crosser still when she saw that the servant who stood by her bedside was not her Ayah.

"Why did you come?" she said to the strange woman. "I will not let you stay. Send my Ayah to me."

The woman looked frightened, but she only stammered that the Ayah could not come and when Mary threw herself into a passion and beat and kicked her, she looked only more frightened and repeated that it was not possible for the Ayah to come to Missie Sahib.

There was something mysterious in the air that morning. Nothing was done in its regular order and several of the native servants seemed missing, while those whom

© GREAT SOURCE. ALL RIGHTS RESERVED.

NAME FOR USE WITH PAGES 315–339

from *The Secret Garden* by Frances Hodgson Burnett, continued

Mary saw slunk or hurried about with ashy and scared faces. But no one would tell her anything and her Ayah did not come. She was actually left alone as the morning went on, and at last she wandered out into the garden and began to play by herself under a tree near the veranda. She pretended that she was making a flowerbed, and she stuck big scarlet hibiscus blossoms into little heaps of earth, all the time growing more and more angry and muttering to herself the things she would say and the names she would call Saidie when she returned.

"Pig! Pig! Daughter of Pigs!" she said, because to call a native a pig is the worst insult of all.

She was grinding her teeth and saying this over and over again when she heard her mother come out on the veranda with some one. She was with a fair young man and they stood talking together in low strange voices. Mary knew the fair young man who looked like a boy. She had heard that he was a very young officer who had just come from England. The child stared at him, but she stared most at her mother. She always did this when she had a chance to see her, because the Mem Sahib—Mary used to call her that oftener than anything else—was such a tall, slim, pretty person and wore such lovely clothes. Her hair was like curly silk and she had a delicate little nose which seemed to be disdaining things, and she had large laughing eyes. All her clothes were thin and floating, and Mary said they were "full of lace." They looked fuller of lace than ever this morning, but her eyes were not laughing at all. They were large and scared and lifted imploringly to the fair boy officer's face.

"Is it so very bad? Oh, is it?" Mary heard her say.

"Awfully," the young man answered in a trembling voice. "Awfully, Mrs. Lennox. You ought to have gone to the hills two weeks ago."

The Mem Sahib wrung her hands.

"Oh, I know I ought!" she cried. "I only stayed to go to that silly dinner party. What a fool I was!"

Stop and Record

Make some notes in the "Characters" section of the Fiction Organizer (page 131). Who will probably be the main character? What is this person like?

At that very moment such a loud sound of wailing broke out from the servants' quarters that she clutched the young man's arm, and Mary stood shivering from head to foot. The wailing grew wilder and wilder.

"What is it? What is it?" Mrs. Lennox gasped.

Fiction

© GREAT SOURCE. ALL RIGHTS RESERVED.

from *The Secret Garden* by Frances Hodgson Burnett, continued

"Some one has died," answered the boy officer. "You did not say it had broken out among your servants."

"I did not know!" the Mem Sahib cried. "Come with me! Come with me!" and she turned and ran into the house.

After that, appalling things happened, and the mysteriousness of the morning was explained to Mary. The cholera had broken out in its most fatal form and people were dying like flies. The Ayah had been taken ill in the night, and it was because she had just died that the servants had wailed in the huts. Before the next day three other servants were dead and others had run away in terror. There was panic on every side, and dying people in all the bungalows.

During the confusion and bewilderment of the second day Mary hid herself in the nursery and was forgotten by everyone. Nobody thought of her, nobody wanted her, and strange things happened of which she knew nothing. Mary alternately cried and slept through the hours. She only knew that people were ill and that she heard mysterious and frightening sounds. Once she crept into the dining room and found it empty, though a partly finished meal was on the table and chairs and plates looked as if they had been hastily pushed back when the diners rose suddenly for some reason. The child ate some fruit and biscuits, and being thirsty she drank a glass of wine which stood nearly filled. It was sweet, and she did not know how strong it was. Very soon it made her intensely drowsy, and she went back to her nursery and shut herself in again, frightened by cries she heard in the huts and by the hurrying sound of feet. The wine made her so sleepy that she could scarcely keep her eyes open and she lay down on her bed and knew nothing more for a long time.

Many things happened during the hours in which she slept so heavily, but she was not disturbed by the wails and the sound of things being carried in and out of the bungalow.

When she awakened she lay and stared at the wall. The house was perfectly still. She had never known it to be so silent before. She heard neither voices nor footsteps, and wondered if everybody had got well of the cholera and all the trouble was over. She wondered also who would take care of her now her Ayah was dead. There would be a new Ayah, and perhaps she would know some new stories. Mary had been rather tired of the old ones. She did not cry because her nurse had died. She was not an affectionate child and had never cared much for anyone. The noise and hurrying about and wailing over the cholera had frightened her, and she had been angry because no one seemed to remember that she was alive. Everyone was too panic-stricken to think of a little girl no one was fond of. When people had the cholera it seemed that they remembered nothing but themselves. But if everyone had got well again, surely someone would remember and come to look for her.

But no one came, and as she lay waiting the house seemed to grow more and more silent. She heard something rustling on the matting and when she looked down she saw

© GREAT SOURCE. ALL RIGHTS RESERVED.

NAME

from *The Secret Garden* by Frances Hodgson Burnett, continued

a little snake gliding along and watching her with eyes like jewels. She was not frightened, because he was a harmless little thing who would not hurt her and he seemed in a hurry to get out of the room. He slipped under the door as she watched him.

"How queer and quiet it is," she said. "It sounds as if there were no one in the bungalow but me and the snake."

Almost the next minute she heard footsteps in the compound, and then on the veranda. They were men's footsteps, and the men entered the bungalow and talked in low voices. No one went to meet or speak to them and they seemed to open doors and look into rooms.

"What desolation!" she heard one voice say. "That pretty, pretty woman! I suppose the child, too. I heard there was a child, though no one ever saw her."

Mary was standing in the middle of the nursery when they opened the door a few minutes later. She looked an ugly, cross little thing and was frowning because she was beginning to be hungry and feel disgracefully neglected. The first man who came in was a large officer she had once seen talking to her father. He looked tired and troubled, but when he saw her he was so startled that he almost jumped back.

"Barney!" he cried out. "There is a child here! A child alone! In a place like this! Mercy on us, who is she?"

"I am Mary Lennox," the little girl said, drawing herself up stiffly. She thought the man was very rude to call her father's bungalow "A place like this!" "I fell asleep when everyone had the cholera and I have only just wakened up. Why does nobody come?"

"It is the child no one ever saw!" exclaimed the man, turning to his companions. "She has actually been forgotten!"

"Why was I forgotten?" Mary said, stamping her foot. "Why does nobody come?"

The young man whose name was Barney looked at her very sadly. Mary even thought she saw him wink his eyes as if to wink tears away.

"Poor little kid!" he said. "There is nobody left to come."

It was in that strange and sudden way that Mary found out that she had neither father nor mother left; that they had died and been carried away in the night, and that the few native servants who had not died also had left the house as quickly as they could get out of it, none of them even remembering that there was a Missie Sahib. That was why the place was so quiet. It was true that there was no one in the bungalow but herself and the little rustling snake.

Stop and Record

Make some notes in the "Plot" section of the Fiction Organizer (page 131). What problem is introduced in the first chapter?

© GREAT SOURCE. ALL RIGHTS RESERVED.

Using the Strategy

You can use the strategy of synthesizing to help you zero in on one major element. For example, you can look at the point of view, the theme, or the writing style.

- **Use the strategy of synthesizing to understand one of the novel's themes.**

An important topic in *The Secret Garden* is loneliness. A Topic and Theme Organizer like the one below helps you explore this topic and what the author says about it.

Directions: Make notes about what the characters say or do in *The Secret Garden*. Your notes should be about the topic of loneliness.

Topic and Theme Organizer

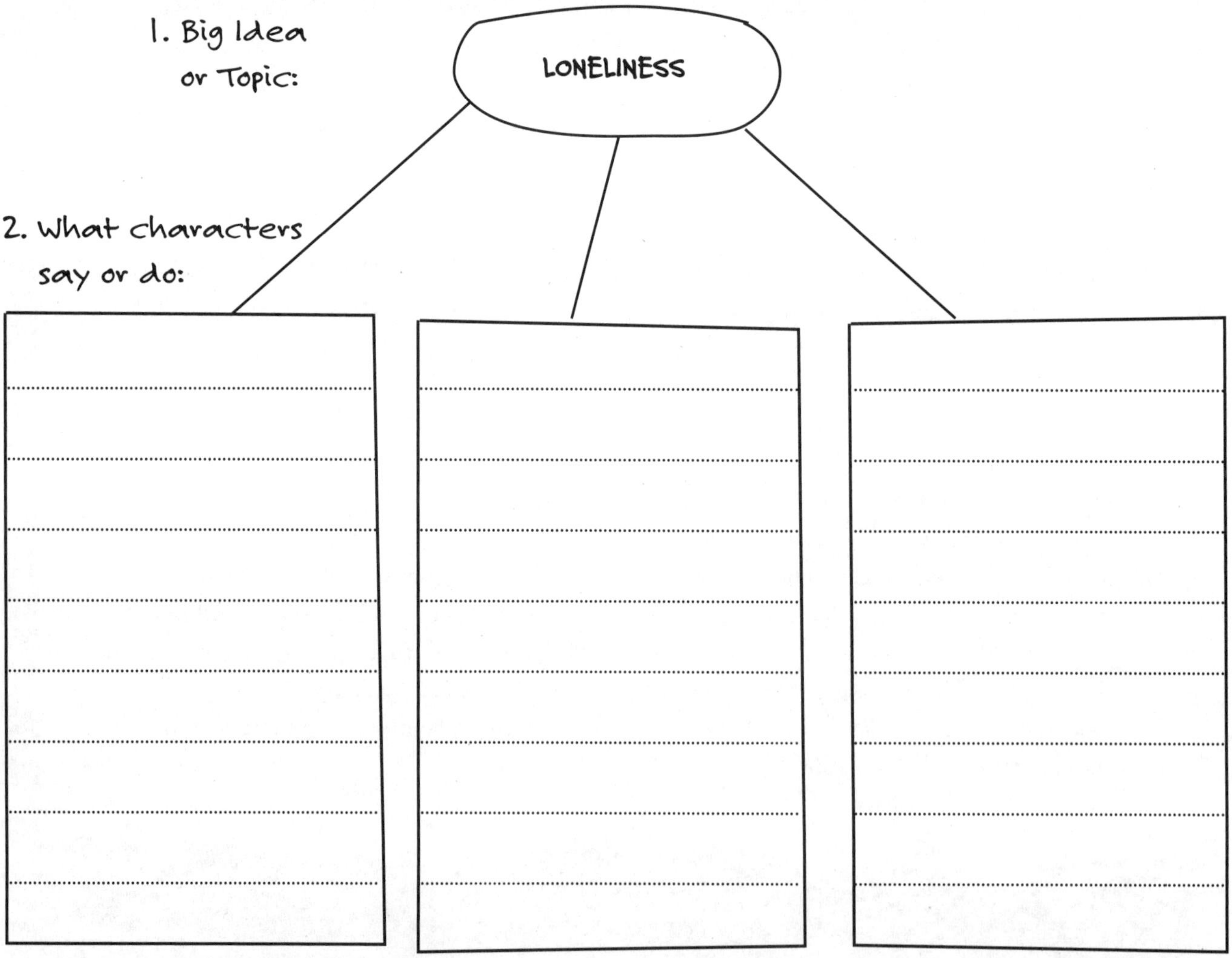

Now you're ready to make some notes in the "Theme" section of the Fiction Organizer (page 131).

© GREAT SOURCE. ALL RIGHTS RESERVED.

NAME FOR USE WITH PAGES 315–339

Understanding How Novels Are Organized

The plot of most novels follows chronological (time) order.

- **You can use a Story String to keep track of the sequence of events the author describes.**

Use this Story String to show what happens in the first chapter of *The Secret Garden*.

Story String

1. Ayah becomes sick when Mary is nine.

2.

3.

4.

5.

Fiction

© GREAT SOURCE. ALL RIGHTS RESERVED.

E Connect

Active readers make connections between characters and events in a novel and their own lives.

- **Making connections with a novel means recording your thoughts and feelings about the text.**

Directions: Here is a Double-entry Journal. Read the quotes from the novel in the left-hand column. Tell how they make you feel in the right-hand column.

Double-entry Journal

Quotes	My Feelings
"So when she was a sickly, fretful, ugly little baby she was kept out of the way, and when she became a sickly, fretful, toddling thing she was kept out of the way also."	
"During the confusion and bewilderment of the second day Mary hid herself in the nursery and was forgotten by everyone."	
"'Why was I forgotten?' Mary said, stamping her foot. 'Why does nobody come?'"	

© GREAT SOURCE. ALL RIGHTS RESERVED.

NAME FOR USE WITH PAGES 315–339

After Reading

After you finish a novel, take a few minutes to think about, digest, and sum up what you've learned.

F Pause and Reflect

Before reading, you set a purpose by asking questions about the six major elements of a novel. Now think back on your reading.

• Ask yourself, "How well did I meet my purpose?"

Directions: If you feel you understand how the element works in the first chapter of the novel, circle *do* in column 2. If you need to read more of the novel before understanding the element, circle *do not*. Then write what you need to understand better.

Element	I understand it very well.	What I need to understand better:
Point of view	do do not	
Characters	do do not	
Setting	do do not	
Plot	do do not	
Theme	do do not	
Style	do do not	

G Reread

At the rereading stage, focus on one or more of the major elements. Create a graphic organizer that can help you process what you've read.

• Use graphic organizers to process information from the novel.

© GREAT SOURCE. ALL RIGHTS RESERVED.

NAME

Directions: Reread parts of the chapter that tell about Mary. Write what you know about her on this Character Map.

Character Map

WHAT SHE SAYS AND DOES	WHAT OTHERS THINK ABOUT HER

Mary Lennox

HOW SHE FEELS ABOUT OTHERS	HOW I FEEL ABOUT HER

H Remember

Good readers remember what they've read.

• To remember a novel, give it a rating and then explain your opinion.

Directions: Rate Chapter 1 of *The Secret Garden*. Then explain your opinion.

Plot

1 2 3 4 5 6 7 8 9 10

Dull — Interesting — Very Interesting

Characters

1 2 3 4 5 6 7 8 9 10

Not Believable — Somewhat Believable — Very Believable

Setting

1 2 3 4 5 6 7 8 9 10

Not Developed — Somewhat Developed — Well Developed

Why I gave the ratings I did:

© GREAT SOURCE. ALL RIGHTS RESERVED.

NAME

FOR USE WITH PAGES 340–350

Focus on Characters

Understanding a story's characters can help you understand plot, other characters, and the theme. Use the following steps to analyze a character.

Step 1: Make notes on what the character does and says.

Directions: Read this excerpt from the story "The Reluctant Dragon." Highlight what the dragon *does*. Underline what he *says*.

from "The Reluctant Dragon" by Kenneth Grahame

Next day, after he'd had his tea, the Boy strolled up the chalky track that led to the summit of the Downs; and there, sure enough, he found the dragon, stretched lazily on the sward in front of his cave. . . .

"Hullo, dragon!" said the Boy, quietly, when he had got up to him.

The dragon, on hearing the approaching footsteps, made the beginning of a courteous effort to rise. But when he saw it was a Boy, he set his eyebrows severely.

"Now don't you hit me," he said; "or bung stones, or squirt water, or anything. I won't have it, I tell you!"

"Not goin' to hit you," said the Boy wearily, dropping on the grass beside the beast. "And don't, for goodness' sake, keep on saying 'Don't'; I hear so much of it, and it's monotonous, and makes me tired. I've simply looked in to ask you how you were and all that sort of thing; but if I'm in the way I can easily clear out. I've lots of friends, and no one can say I'm in the habit of shoving myself in where I'm not wanted!"

"No, no, don't go off in a huff," said the dragon, hastily; "fact is, I'm as happy up here as the day's long; never without an occupation, dear fellow, never without an occupation! And yet, between ourselves, it *is* a trifle dull at times."

The Boy bit off a stalk of grass and chewed it. "Going to make a long stay here?" he asked, politely.

"Can't hardly say at present," replied the dragon. "It seems a nice place enough—but I've only been here a short time, and one must look about and reflect and consider before settling down. It's rather a serious thing, settling down. Besides—now I'm going to tell you something! You'd never guess it if you tried ever so!—fact is, I'm such a confoundedly lazy beggar!"

Fiction

© GREAT SOURCE. ALL RIGHTS RESERVED.

Step 2: Create a Character Map.

Use a Character Map to keep track of facts and details. It will help you draw conclusions about a character.

Directions: Complete this Character Map about the dragon.

Character Map

WHAT HE SAYS AND DOES	WHAT OTHERS THINK ABOUT HIM

CHARACTER'S NAME

HOW HE FEELS ABOUT OTHERS	HOW I FEEL ABOUT HIM

© GREAT SOURCE. ALL RIGHTS RESERVED.

NAME FOR USE WITH PAGES 340–350

Step 3: Draw conclusions about characters.

Next, make inferences, or reasonable guesses, about the character.

Directions: Write your conclusions about the dragon in the column on the right. The first one is done for you.

Inference Chart

What the character does and says	My conclusions about the character
"The dragon, on hearing the approaching footsteps, made the beginning of a courteous effort to rise."	He is polite and has good manners. He is someone I might like.
"'Now don't you hit me,' he said . . ."	
"'. . . I'm as happy up here as the day's long; never without an occupation, dear fellow, never without an occupation!'"	

Fiction

© GREAT SOURCE. ALL RIGHTS RESERVED.

Focus on Setting

Setting can affect a story's mood, characters, and plot. Use the steps outlined here to analyze a setting.

Step 1: Do a close reading and record details.

Directions: Read this excerpt from *The Wonderful Wizard of Oz.* Highlight clues about time of day. Underline clues about place. Use the Setting Chart to keep track of the setting clues you found.

from *The Wonderful Wizard of Oz* by L. Frank Baum

As it was, the jar made her catch her breath and wonder what had happened; and Toto put his cold little nose into her face and whined dismally. Dorothy sat up and noticed that the house was not moving; nor was it dark, for the bright sunshine came in at the window flooding the little room. She sprang from her bed and with Toto at her heels ran and opened the door.

The little girl gave a cry of amazement and looked about her, her eyes growing bigger and bigger at the wonderful sights she saw.

The cyclone had set the house down very gently—for a cyclone—in the midst of a country of marvelous beauty. There were lovely patches of greensward all about, with stately trees bearing rich and luscious fruits. Banks of gorgeous flowers were on every hand, and birds with rare and brilliant plumage sang and fluttered in the trees and bushes. A little way off was a small brook, rushing and sparkling along between green banks, and murmuring in a voice very grateful to a little girl who had lived so long on the dry, gray prairies.

Setting Chart

CLUES ABOUT TIME	CLUES ABOUT PLACE
time of day:	where the story takes place:
season:	what it looks like:

© GREAT SOURCE. ALL RIGHTS RESERVED.

NAME FOR USE WITH PAGES 351–359

Step 2: Draw conclusions about the setting and mood.

The setting can affect the mood, or atmosphere, of a story. For example, a beautiful setting can create a joyful mood. An ugly setting can create a gloomy mood.

Directions: Read the first quote below and write what it shows you about the mood. Then add another quote and write what it shows about the mood.

Double-entry Journal

QUOTE	WHAT THIS TELLS ME ABOUT THE MOOD
". . . her eyes growing bigger and bigger at the wonderful sights she saw."	

Step 3: Draw conclusions about the setting and characters.

Setting can also give you clues about characters. Look for the character's response to the setting.

Directions: Read the first sentence about Dorothy in the Inference Chart. In the second column write what it tells you about her. Then write another sentence about Dorothy. Also write what it tells you about her.

Inference Chart

WHAT DOROTHY SAYS OR DOES	MY INFERENCES ABOUT DOROTHY
Dorothy sprang from her bed.	

Fiction

© GREAT SOURCE. ALL RIGHTS RESERVED.

Focus on Dialogue

When your focus is dialogue, keep a close eye on who is talking, what is being said, and how it is being said. Follow these steps to analyze dialogue.

Step 1: Do a careful reading.

First, read the dialogue slowly and carefully. Make notes as you go.

Directions: Read this excerpt from *Alice in Wonderland*. Make notes on the sticky notes.

from *Alice in Wonderland* by Lewis Carroll

When the procession came opposite to Alice, they all stopped and looked at her, and the Queen said severely, "Who is this?" She said it to the Knave of Hearts, who only bowed and smiled in reply.

1. "Idiot!" said the Queen, tossing her head impatiently; and, turning to Alice, she went on: "What's your name, child?"

"My name is Alice, so please your Majesty," said Alice very politely; but she added to herself, "Why they're only a pack of cards, after all. I needn't be afraid of them!"

"And who are these?" said the Queen, pointing to the three gardeners who were lying around the rose tree; for, you see, as they were lying on their faces, and the pattern on their backs was the same as the rest of the pack, she could not tell whether they were gardeners, or soldiers, or courtiers, or three of her own children.

2. "How should I know?" said Alice, surprised at her own courage. "It's no business of mine."

The Queen turned crimson with fury, and, after glaring at her for a moment like a wild beast, began screaming, "Off with her head! Off—"

"Nonsense!" said Alice, very loudly and decidedly, and the Queen was silent.

The King laid his hand upon her arm, and timidly said, "Consider, my dear; she is only a child!"

1. The speech tag tells me

2. The speech tag tells me

© GREAT SOURCE. ALL RIGHTS RESERVED.

NAME FOR USE WITH PAGES 360–367

Step 2: Look for clues about character.

Then look for what the dialogue reveals about each character.

Directions: Write your inferences about the Queen, Alice, and the King here. Explain your evidence or "proof."

Inference Chart

CHARACTER	INFERENCES	"PROOF" FROM THE DIALOGUE
Queen		
Alice		
King		

Step 3: Look for clues about plot.

Next, think about the plot. In dialogue, you can often find clues about what's going to happen next.

Directions: Predict what you think will happen next in this scene from *Alice in Wonderland.* Then explain your prediction.

My prediction:

Why I think this will happen:

Step 4: Look for clues about mood.

What the characters say and how they say it can affect a story's mood.

Directions: What is the mood in this scene from *Alice in Wonderland?* Which character or characters help create this mood?

Mood:

Character who creates it:

Fiction

© GREAT SOURCE. ALL RIGHTS RESERVED.

Focus on Plot

Plot is the series of events that connect the beginning of a story to the end. Follow these steps to analyze a plot.

Step 1: Track the key events.

In a well-written plot, one event leads into another like stairs on a staircase.

Directions: Read these events from Hans Christian Andersen's tale "The Ugly Duckling." Number them in the correct order and draw sketches on the Storyboard to show the action.

EVENTS:

___ The ugly duckling runs away.

___ The duckling looks in the water and finds that he, too, is a swan.

___ A mother duck hatches a brood of baby ducks, one of which is large and ugly.

___ In the spring, the duckling sees some swans and expects that they will kill him.

___ The ugly duckling is teased by the barnyard animals.

___ He spends the winter outside and is cold, hungry, and lonely.

Storyboard

1.	2.	3.
4.	5.	6.

© GREAT SOURCE. ALL RIGHTS RESERVED.

NAME .... FOR USE WITH PAGES 368–375

Step 2: Analyze the conflict.

Next, think about the main conflict, or problem, of the plot.

Directions: Read this excerpt from "The Ugly Duckling." Then explain the conflict.

from "The Ugly Duckling" by Hans Christian Andersen

The little ducks made themselves at home in the farmyard, but the poor ugly duckling was bitten, pushed about, and made fun of both by the ducks and the hens. "He is too big," they said. The turkey gobbler puffed himself out until he became very red in the face and flew at the poor little duckling. The duckling was chased by all, and even his brothers and sisters were unkind to him. They would say, "Oh, you ugly creature, I wish the cat would get you." His mother said, "I wish you were miles away."

The conflict is ....

....

Step 3: Think about plot and theme.

Very often the events of the plot will reveal the writer's theme.

Directions: Read the last paragraph from "The Ugly Duckling." Decide on the author's message, or theme. Then write a journal response.

from "The Ugly Duckling" by Hans Christian Andersen

The poor swan was so happy he did not know what to do, but he was not at all proud. He had been hated for being ugly, and now he heard them say that he was the most beautiful of birds. He rustled his feathers, curved his slender neck, and said, "Now, when people see me, they will be glad. I never dreamed of such happiness when I was an ugly duckling."

Journal Response

....

....

© GREAT SOURCE. ALL RIGHTS RESERVED.

Focus on Theme

A writer's message, or main idea, is the theme of a work. Many stories have more than one theme. Sometimes you have to be a bit of a detective to discover them.

Step 1: Find the "big ideas" or general topics.

Sometimes the title or first paragraph of a work will give you a clue about a "big idea" or topic.

Directions: Read these titles. Write what you think are the big ideas on the lines. One has been done for you.

The Secret Garden secrets	*Call It Courage*
Taken in Slavery	"I'm Nobody"

Step 2: Find out what the characters do or say that relates to the general topic.

Next, find details in the text that relate to the big idea you've identified. Begin by thinking about what the characters say and do.

© GREAT SOURCE. ALL RIGHTS RESERVED.

NAME FOR USE WITH PAGES 376–382

Directions: Read the quotes from *The Secret Garden*. Tell how they relate to the big idea of "loneliness."

Double-entry Journal

Quote	What it tells me about loneliness
"She had not wanted a little girl at all, and when Mary was born she handed her over to the care of an Ayah. . . ."	
"She was not an affectionate child and had never cared much for anyone."	
"'There is nobody left to come.'"	

Step 3: Come up with a statement of the author's point or message about the big idea.

Remember that the theme is the point the author wants to make about the topic.

Directions: Complete this Topic and Theme Organizer. Use your notes from Chapter 1 of *The Secret Garden* (pages 132–135).

Topic and Theme Organizer

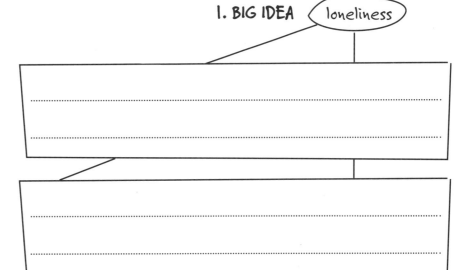

1. BIG IDEA: loneliness

2. WHAT CHARACTERS DO OR SAY

3. WHAT IS IMPORTANT TO LEARN

© GREAT SOURCE. ALL RIGHTS RESERVED.

Focus on Comparing and Contrasting

When you make a general comparison, you compare two works—for example, a poem to a poem or a novel to a novel. When you make a specific comparison, you compare one element in two works—for example, a setting to a setting or a character to a character. Follow these steps to make a comparison of two characters.

Step 1: Read.

Your first step is to read carefully. When you are comparing and contrasting, you look for similarities and differences.

Directions: Read the excerpt from *The Phantom Tollbooth*. Then read the excerpt from *Johnny Tremain*. Make notes about Milo and Johnny.

from *The Phantom Tollbooth* by Norton Juster

There was once a boy named Milo who didn't know what to do with himself—not just sometimes, but always.

When he was in school he longed to be out, and when he was out he longed to be in. On the way he thought about coming home, and coming home he thought about going. Wherever he was he wished he were somewhere else, and when he got there he wondered why he'd bothered. Nothing really interested him—least of all the things that should have.

What I know about Milo:

....

....

....

....

....

from *Johnny Tremain* by Esther Forbes

Johnny was already in leather breeches, pulling on his coarse shirt, tucking in the tails. He was a rather skinny boy, neither large nor small for fourteen. He had a thin, sleep-flushed face, light eyes, a wry mouth, and fair, lank hair. Although two years younger than the swinish Dove, inches shorter, pounds lighter, he knew, and old Mr. Lapham knew, busy Mrs. Lapham knew and her four daughters and Dove and Dusty also knew, that Johnny Tremain was boss of the attic, and almost all of the house.

What I know about Johnny:

....

....

....

....

....

© GREAT SOURCE. ALL RIGHTS RESERVED.

NAME .... FOR USE WITH PAGES 383–388

Step 2: Use a graphic organizer.

Next, make detailed notes about both characters.

Directions: Complete these two Webs. Write words that describe the characters on the spokes.

Webs

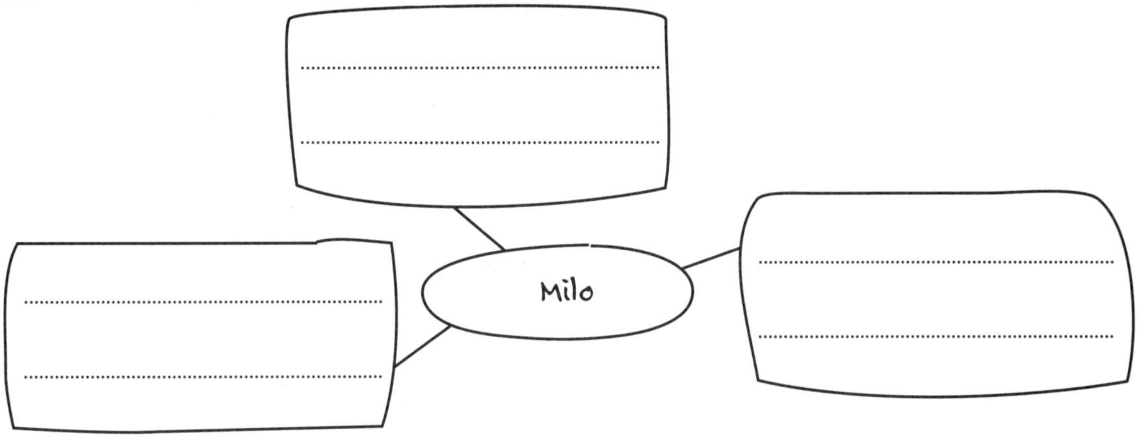

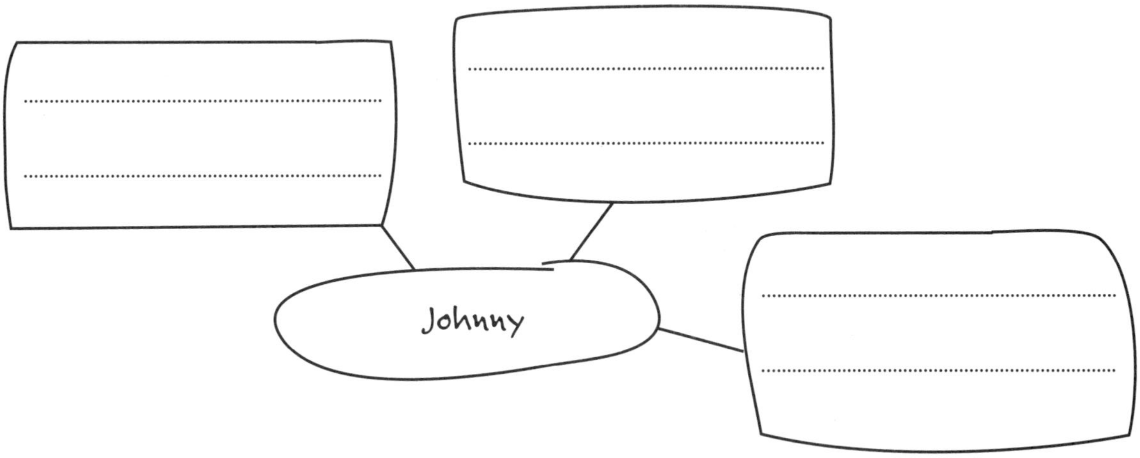

Step 3: Compare and Contrast.

Look for similarities and differences between the two characters.

Directions: Answer these questions about the characters.

How are the two characters similar? ....

....

How are they different? ....

....

© GREAT SOURCE. ALL RIGHTS RESERVED.

Reading a Poem

A poem is like a song. The sound of the words can be as important as the meaning. Good readers of poetry listen for rhythm, look for meaning, and visualize the images.

Before Reading

Use the reading process and the reading strategy of close reading to help you read a famous poem by Henry Wadsworth Longfellow.

A Set a Purpose

Your purpose for reading a poem has two parts: find out what the poem is about and learn what it means.

- **Ask questions about the subject and meaning of the poem.**

Directions: Write your purpose for reading "Paul Revere's Ride" below. Then predict who and what you think the poem will be about.

My purpose: ....

....

My prediction: ....

....

B Preview

Always begin with a preview. Read the title and name of the poet. Look at the structure and the overall shape of the poem on the page. Read the first and last lines.

Directions: Make notes on the chart on the next page.

© GREAT SOURCE. ALL RIGHTS RESERVED.

NAME

FOR USE WITH PAGES 408-421

Paul Revere's Ride

by Henry Wadsworth Longfellow

The title of the poem: ....

The poet's name: ....

I noticed this about the overall shape of the poem: ....

....

....

....

The first and last lines suggest this: ....

....

....

....

© GREAT SOURCE. ALL RIGHTS RESERVED.

"Paul Revere's Ride" by Henry Wadsworth Longfellow

Listen, my children, and you shall hear
Of the midnight ride of Paul Revere,
On the eighteenth of April, in Seventy-five;
Hardly a man is now alive
Who remembers that famous day and year.

He said to his friend, "If the British march
By land or sea from the town tonight,
Hang a lantern aloft in the belfry arch
Of the North Church tower as a signal light,—
One, if by land, and two, if by sea;
And I on the opposite shore will be,
Ready to ride and spread the alarm
Through every Middlesex village and farm
For the country folk to be up and to arm."

Then he said, "Good night!" and with muffled oar
Silently rowed to the Charlestown shore,
Just as the moon rose over the bay,
Where swinging wide at her moorings lay
The *Somerset*, British man-of-war;
A phantom ship, with each mast and spar
Across the moon like a prison bar,
And a huge black hulk, that was magnified
By its own reflection in the tide.

Meanwhile, his friend, through alley and street,
Wanders and watches with eager ears,
Till in the silence around him he hears
The muster of men at the barrack door,
The sound of arms, and the tramp of feet,
And the measured tread of the grenadiers,
Marching down to their boats on the shore.

© GREAT SOURCE. ALL RIGHTS RESERVED.

NAME

"Paul Revere's Ride" by Henry Wadsworth Longfellow, continued

Then he climbed the tower of the Old North Church,
By the wooden stairs, with stealthy tread,
To the belfry-chamber overhead,
And startled the pigeons from their perch
On the sombre rafters, that round him made
Masses and moving shapes of shade,—
By the trembling ladder, steep and tall,
To the highest window in the wall,
Where he paused to listen and look down
A moment on the roofs of the town,
And the moonlight flowing over all.

Beneath, in the churchyard, lay the dead,
In their night-encampment on the hill,
Wrapped in silence so deep and still
That he could hear, like a sentinel's tread,
The watchful night wind, as it went
Creeping along from tent to tent,
And seeming to whisper, "All is well!"
A moment only he feels the spell
Of the place and the hour, and the secret dread
Of the lonely belfry and the dead;
For suddenly all his thoughts are bent
On a shadowy something far away,
Where the river widens to meet the bay,—
A line of black that bends and floats
On the rising tide, like a bridge of boats.

Meanwhile, impatient to mount and ride,
Booted and spurred, with a heavy stride
On the opposite shore walked Paul Revere.
Now he patted his horse's side,
Now gazed at the landscape far and near,
Then, impetuous, stamped the earth,
And turned and tightened his saddle-girth;
But mostly he watched with eager search
The belfry-tower of the Old North Church,
As it rose above the graves on the hill,

© GREAT SOURCE. ALL RIGHTS RESERVED.

Lonely and spectral and sombre and still.
And lo! as he looks, on the belfry's height
A glimmer, and then a gleam of light!
He springs to the saddle, the bridle he turns,
But lingers and gazes, till full on his sight
A second lamp in the belfry burns!

A hurry of hoofs in a village street,
A shape in the moonlight, a bulk in the dark,
And beneath, from the pebbles, in passing, a spark
Struck out by a steed flying fearless and fleet:
That was all! And yet, through the gloom and the light,
The fate of a nation was riding that night;
And the spark struck out by that steed, in his flight,
Kindled the land into flame with its heat.

He has left the village and mounted the steep,
And beneath him, tranquil and broad and deep,
Is the Mystic, meeting the ocean tides;
And under the alders, that skirt its edge,
Now soft on the sand, now loud on the ledge,
Is heard the tramp of his steed as he rides.

It was twelve by the village clock
When he crossed the bridge into Medford town.
He heard the crowing of the cock,
And the barking of the farmer's dog,
And felt the damp of the river fog,
That rises after the sun goes down.

It was one by the village clock,
When he galloped into Lexington.
He saw the gilded weathercock
Swim in the moonlight as he passed,
And the meeting-house windows, blank and bare,
Gaze at him with a spectral glare,
As if they already stood aghast
At the bloody work they would look upon.

© GREAT SOURCE. ALL RIGHTS RESERVED.

NAME

"Paul Revere's Ride" by Henry Wadsworth Longfellow, continued

It was two by the village clock,
When he came to the bridge in Concord town.
He heard the bleating of the flock,
And the twitter of birds among the trees,
And felt the breath of the morning breeze
Blowing over the meadows brown.
And one was safe and asleep in his bed
Who at the bridge would be first to fall,
Who that day would be lying dead,
Pierced by a British musket ball.

You know the rest. In the books you have read,
How the British Regulars fired and fled,—
How the farmers gave them ball for ball,
From behind each fence and farmyard wall,
Chasing the redcoats down the lane,
Then crossing the fields to emerge again
Under the trees at the turn of the road,
And only pausing to fire and load.

So through the night rode Paul Revere;
And so through the night went his cry of alarm
To every Middlesex village and farm,—
A cry of defiance and not of fear,
A voice in the darkness, a knock at the door,
And a word that shall echo forevermore!
For, borne on the night wind of the Past,
Through all our history, to the last,
In the hour of darkness and peril and need,
The people will waken and listen to hear
The hurrying hoofbeats of that steed,
And the midnight message of Paul Revere.

© GREAT SOURCE. ALL RIGHTS RESERVED.

C Plan

Your preview has given you a lot to think about. You need a plan that can help you get more from your reading of Longfellow's poem. Try using the strategy of close reading. To do that, you'll need to read the poem at least three times.

- **Use the strategy of close reading with poetry.**

During Reading

D Read with a Purpose

On your first reading, read for enjoyment. On your second reading, read for meaning. On your third reading, read for structure, or elements of poetry such as rhyme scheme and imagery.

Directions: Read Longfellow's poem three times. After each reading, make notes in the chart.

First Reading	Second Reading	Third Reading
Here's what I liked about the poem:	I think Longfellow's message is this:	Here's what I noticed about the structure:

© GREAT SOURCE. ALL RIGHTS RESERVED.

NAME .... FOR USE WITH PAGES 408-421

Using the Strategy

The best strategy to use with a poem is a close reading. This means reading word for word, line for line. Create a Double-entry Journal. It can help you respond to individual lines of the poem.

- **Use a Double-entry Journal to organize your thoughts about the poem.**

Directions: Read the quotes from Longfellow's poem. Write what you think the words mean or how they make you feel in the right column.

Double-entry Journal

Quote	My thoughts about it
"And lo! as he looks, on the belfry's height A glimmer, and then a gleam of light!"	
"A voice in the darkness, a knock at the door, And a word that shall echo forevermore!"	

Understanding How Poems Are Organized

Understanding how a poem is organized can help you search for meaning.

Directions: Do a close reading of the stanza that follows. Then complete the sticky notes.

Poetry

© GREAT SOURCE. ALL RIGHTS RESERVED.

from "Paul Revere's Ride" by Henry Wadsworth Longfellow

Then he climbed the tower of the Old North Church,
By the wooden stairs, with stealthy tread,
To the belfry-chamber overhead,
And startled the pigeons from their perch
On the sombre rafters, that round him made
Masses and moving shapes of shade,—
By the trembling ladder, steep and tall,
To the highest window in the wall,
Where he paused to listen and look down
A moment on the roofs of the town,
And the moonlight flowing over all.

The rhyme follows a regular / irregular pattern.

Examples of rhyme are ....

The image seen from the highest window is ....

E Connect

Making a personal connection can help you understand the poet's meaning.

• Record how the poem makes you feel.

Directions: Reread the final stanza of "Paul Revere's Ride" on page 159. Tell how the words make you feel.

© GREAT SOURCE. ALL RIGHTS RESERVED.

NAME

FOR USE WITH PAGES 408-421

After Reading

Take a moment to collect your thoughts about "Paul Revere's Ride."

F Pause and Reflect

Return to your reading purpose. Ask yourself, "Do I know what the poem is about? Do I know what it means? Do I remember any particular words?"

Directions: Tell why you have, or have not, met your reading purpose.

G Reread

Use the rereading strategy of paraphrasing to zero in on individual lines from the poem.

- **A powerful rereading strategy to use is paraphrasing.**

Directions: Read the lines in the column on the left. Write a paraphrase of the lines in the column on the right. One has been done for you.

Poetry

Paraphrase Chart

Quote	My thoughts about it
"A hurry of hoofs in a village street, A shape in the moonlight, a bulk in the dark"	Someone is moving about the city secretly, on horseback.
"And the meeting-house windows, blank and bare"	
"You know the rest. In the books you have read, How the British Regulars fired and fled"	

© GREAT SOURCE. ALL RIGHTS RESERVED.

H Remember

Good readers remember what they've read.

- **Making a sketch can help you remember what you've read.**

Directions: Make a sketch of "Paul Revere's Ride." Then write a caption underneath.

Caption:

© GREAT SOURCE. ALL RIGHTS RESERVED.

NAME FOR USE WITH PAGES 422-429

Focus on Language

Poets make every word count. Your job as reader is to examine the language the poet uses and see how it affects the meaning of the poem. Follow these steps.

Step 1: Read and take notes.

Directions: Read the following stanzas from a poem the whole way through without stopping. Then read them a second time. Use a highlighter to mark difficult words and unusual phrases.

from "Annabel Lee" by Edgar Allan Poe

It was many and many a year ago,
In a kingdom by the sea,
That a maiden there lived whom you may know
By the name of Annabel Lee;—
And this maiden she lived with no other thought
Than to love and be loved by me.

I was a child and *She* was a child,
In this kingdom by the sea,
But we loved with a love that was more than love—
I and my Annabel Lee—
With a love that the wingèd seraphs[1] of Heaven
Coveted her and me.

And this was the reason that, long ago,
In this kingdom by the sea,
A wind blew out of a cloud by night,
Chilling my Annabel Lee;
So that her high-born kinsmen came
And bore her away from me,
To shut her up in a sepulchre[2]
In this kingdom by the sea.

[1] **seraphs**, angels.

[2] **sepulchre**, burial vault.

Poetry

© GREAT SOURCE. ALL RIGHTS RESERVED.

Step 2: Find key words.

Your next step is to read the poem a third time. This time watch for key words, including words that describe an action, create a mood, or name a person, place, or thing.

Directions: Reread the poem, one line at a time. Try using a Two Per Line to find key words. This means going back to the poem and circling the two most important words in each line. Choose the important words and write them below.

I think these are the most important words in Poe's poem: ....

....

Step 3: Look for figurative language and imagery.

Poets often use words in new ways. They use figurative language (words that create pictures in a reader's mind) and imagery (words that appeal to the five senses). This brings freshness to their writing.

Directions: Read the phrases on this chart. They are examples of figurative language and imagery in "Annabel Lee." Tell about the picture created by the phrases and how they make you feel.

Phrase from the Poem	Picture Created	How It Makes Me Feel
"In a kingdom by the sea"		
"But we loved with a love that was more than love"		
"A wind blew out of a cloud"		

© GREAT SOURCE. ALL RIGHTS RESERVED.

NAME

FOR USE WITH PAGES 430-438

Focus on Meaning

When you read a poem, it's natural to try to figure out what it means. Use the reading process and the strategy of close reading to help you understand the poet's "message" for readers.

Step 1: Look for clues to meaning.

First, read the poem the whole way through without stopping. Try to get an idea of what it is about. Then read the poem again. Make notes about important or interesting words.

Directions: Read this poem by Emily Dickinson. Make notes.

"I'm Nobody" by Emily Dickinson

I'm nobody! Who are you?
Are you nobody, too?
Then there's a pair of us—don't tell!
They'd banish us, you know.

How dreary to be somebody!
How public, like a frog
To tell your name the livelong day
To an admiring bog!

I noticed this about the title:

A bog must be like:

The word dreary makes me feel like this:

Poetry

© GREAT SOURCE. ALL RIGHTS RESERVED.

Step 2: Consider what's unusual and important.

Use the reading strategy of close reading to help you understand what the poem means. Reread the poem line by line. Look for unusual and important lines or ideas. Then write what you think of them.

Directions: Record your responses to important lines from the poem. Start with the line given. Then add two more lines and your responses to them.

Double-entry Journal

Unusual/Important Lines	My Thoughts
"I'm nobody! Who are you?"	

Step 3: Explore your feelings.

Note your personal responses to a poem. They can help you explore meaning.

Directions: Answer these questions. Refer to your notes as needed.

What did you picture when you were reading the poem?

What does the title of the poem remind you of?

© GREAT SOURCE. ALL RIGHTS RESERVED.

NAME ....

FOR USE WITH PAGES 430-438

Step 4: Decide what the poet is saying.

Finish by figuring out what the poet is trying to say. What message does the poem have for readers? Use this formula to help you figure out the message.

Topic of "I'm Nobody"	+	What Dickinson says about it	=	Poem's message
....	+	....	=	....
....		....		....
....		....		....

Directions: Paraphrase, or retell, parts of the poem. Write your notes in the Paraphrase Chart.

Paraphrase Chart

Quote	My Paraphrase
"Then there's a pair of us—don't tell! They'd banish us, you know."	
"How dreary to be somebody!"	
"How public, like a frog To tell your name the livelong day To an admiring bog!"	

© GREAT SOURCE. ALL RIGHTS RESERVED.

Poetry

Focus on Sound and Structure

Focusing on sound and structure can increase your enjoyment and understanding of a poem. Follow these steps.

Step 1: Examine the Organization.

Begin by reading just for fun, to get an idea of what's there. Then take a moment to examine how the poem looks on the page.

Directions: Read these lines from "The Jumblies," a poem by Edward Lear. Write your ideas on the sticky notes.

from "The Jumblies" by Edward Lear

They went to sea in a sieve, they did;
In a sieve they went to sea:
In spite of all their friends could say,
On a winter's morn, on a stormy day,
In a sieve they went to sea.
And when the sieve turned round and round,
And every one cried, "you'll all be drowned!"
They called aloud, "Our sieve ain't big,
But we don't care a button, we don't care a fig:
In a sieve we'll go to sea!"
Far and few, far and few, a
Are the lands where the Jumblies live: b
Their heads are green, and their hands are blue; a
And they went to sea in a sieve. b

I noticed this about the words:

I noticed this about the way the lines look:

© GREAT SOURCE. ALL RIGHTS RESERVED.

NAME .... FOR USE WITH PAGES 439–445

Step 2: Look for repeated words and sounds.

Next, listen for the "music" of a poem. What do the words *sound* like?

Directions: Reread the lines from "The Jumblies." Highlight repeated words. Then write what you noticed in this chart.

Examples of Repeated Words	Examples of Repeated Sounds

Step 3: Listen to the rhyme.

Always listen for rhyme. It contributes to the overall effect of the poem. Rhyme usually appears at the end of the lines. You can use lowercase letters to show the rhyme pattern. For example:

from "The Jumblies" by Edward Lear

They went to sea in a sieve, they did; a
In a sieve they went to sea: b
In spite of all their friends could say, c
On a winter's morn, on a stormy day, c

Directions: Return to the poem in Step 1. Use lowercase letters to show the rhyme scheme of the last four lines. Write the letters next to these lines.

Step 4: Hear the rhythm or meter.

Can you hear the rhythm, or beat, Edward Lear uses in "The Jumblies"?

Directions: Whisper the poem aloud to yourself. Then write about the rhythm. Hint: Does the poem sound like a rocking boat, a battle cry, and a lullaby?

Here's why: ....

....

© GREAT SOURCE. ALL RIGHTS RESERVED.

Reading a Play

The entire action of a play is told through dialogue and stage directions. This means that when you read a play, you need to stay alert and really listen to what the characters say.

Before Reading

Practice reading a play here. Use the reading process and the strategy of summarizing to help you get *more* from a scene based on the well-known book *A Christmas Carol.*

A Set a Purpose

Your purpose for reading a play is to find out about the characters, conflict, and theme.

- **To set your purpose, ask a question about the characters, conflict, and theme of the play.**

Directions: Write your purpose for reading *A Christmas Carol* here. Then tell what you already know about this story.

My purpose: ....

....

....

....

....

What I know: ....

....

....

....

© GREAT SOURCE. ALL RIGHTS RESERVED.

NAME FOR USE WITH PAGES 472-488

B Preview

It's important to preview a play before you begin reading. Look for information that relates to your purpose.

- **Previewing a play beforehand helps you know what to expect during your careful reading.**

Directions: Preview the title page and first several lines of *A Christmas Carol* (pages 173–174). Write your ideas on the sticky notes.

A Christmas Carol

A Play Based on the Novel
by Charles Dickens

Characters, in order of appearance

Ebeneezer Scrooge
Bob Cratchit
Fred, Scrooge's nephew
Two Gentlemen collecting for the Poor and Destitute
Jacob Marley's Ghost
The Ghosts of Christmas Past, Christmas Present, and Christmas Yet to Come
Mrs. Cratchit
Tiny Tim and the other Cratchit children
Various minor characters

Setting

Christmas Eve, during the mid- to late 1800s, in London

Here's what I noticed after skimming the first several lines.

The title of the play is

The first three characters in the cast are

Drama

© GREAT SOURCE. ALL RIGHTS RESERVED.

Act I, Scene 1

*(*SCROOGE *is in his office. He keeps his eye on his clerk,* BOB CRATCHIT, *who is copying letters. There is a small fire near* SCROOGE *and an even smaller one near* BOB CRATCHIT. *Suddenly, the door flies open and in steps Scrooge's nephew,* FRED.)

FRED *(Cheerfully)*. Merry Christmas, Uncle!

SCROOGE *(In a grumpy voice)*. Bah! Humbug!

FRED *(Glowing from his walk in the fog and frost)*. Christmas a humbug, Uncle? You don't mean that, I'm sure.

SCROOGE. I do. Merry Christmas! What reason have you to be merry? You're poor enough.

FRED *(Pleasantly)*. What reason have you to be unhappy? You're rich enough.

SCROOGE *(Having no better answer on the spur of the moment)*. Bah! Humbug!

FRED. Don't be cross.

SCROOGE. What else can I be when I live in a world of fools.

FRED. Uncle!

SCROOGE *(Sternly)*. Nephew! Keep Christmas in your own way, and let me keep it in mine!

FRED. Keep it! But you don't keep it at all.

SCROOGE. Let me leave it alone, then. Much good it has ever done.

FRED. There are many things that are good but not profitable, Christmas among them. I have always thought of Christmas as a good time. It is a kind, forgiving, charitable, pleasant time. Though it has never put a scrap of gold or silver in my pocket, I believe that it has done me good, and will do me good.

(At this point BOB CRATCHIT *applauds. Then he becomes immediately aware that* SCROOGE *is watching him, so he pokes the small fire, putting out the last spark.)*

SCROOGE *(Speaking to* BOB CRATCHIT*)*. Let me hear another sound from you and you'll keep your Christmas by losing your position!

FRED. Don't be angry, Uncle. Come and dine with us tomorrow.

SCROOGE. Good afternoon!

Stop and Record

Fill in the "Characters" and "Setting" boxes of your Fiction Organizer (page 177).

© GREAT SOURCE. ALL RIGHTS RESERVED.

NAME

FOR USE WITH PAGES 472-488

from *A Christmas Carol*, continued

(FRED leaves the room without an angry word. He stops at the door to say "Merry Christmas" to BOB CRATCHIT, who returns the greeting cordially. The clerk in letting FRED out has let two other people in. They stand, with their hats off, in Scrooge's office.)

FIRST GENTLEMAN *(Looking at a piece of paper)*. Scrooge and Marley's, I believe. Have I the pleasure of addressing Mr. Scrooge or Mr. Marley?

SCROOGE. Mr. Marley has been dead these seven years. He died seven years ago, this very night.

SECOND GENTLEMAN *(Presenting his credentials)*. We have no doubt his generosity is well represented by his surviving partner.

(At the word generosity *SCROOGE frowns, shakes his head, and hands the credentials back to the SECOND GENTLEMAN.)*

FIRST GENTLEMAN *(Holding up a pen)*. At this festive season of the year, Mr. Scrooge, it is often desirable to make a donation for the Poor and Destitute. Many thousands are in need of the basic necessities. Hundreds of thousands are in need of common comforts.

SCROOGE. Are there no prisons?

FIRST GENTLEMAN*(Putting down the pen)*. Plenty of prisons.

SCROOGE *(In a demanding voice)*. The workhouses? Are they still operating?

SECOND GENTLEMAN. They are still. I wish I could say they were not.

SCROOGE. Oh! I was afraid, from what you said at first, that something had happened to stop them from their usefulness.

SECOND GENTLEMAN. We believe they scarcely offer cheer of mind or body. A few of us are trying to raise money to buy the Poor and Destitute some meat and drink. What shall I put you down for?

SCROOGE. Nothing.

FIRST GENTLEMAN. You wish to be anonymous?

SCROOGE. I wish to be left alone. I don't make merry myself at Christmas and I can't afford to make idle people merry. I help to support the establishments I have mentioned. They cost enough. Those who are badly off must go there.

© GREAT SOURCE. ALL RIGHTS RESERVED.

from *A Christmas Carol*, continued

FIRST GENTLEMAN. Many can't go there. Many would rather die.

SCROOGE. If they would rather die, they had better do it and decrease the surplus population. Besides, I don't know that.

SECOND GENTLEMAN. But you might know it.

SCROOGE. It's not my business. It's enough for a man to understand his own business. Mine occupies me constantly. Good afternoon, gentlemen.

(Seeing that it will be useless to pursue the point, the GENTLEMAN *leave. Scrooge returns to his work with a good opinion of himself.)*

Stop and Record

Fill in the "Plot" box of your Fiction Organizer (page 177).

C Plan

Next make a plan. What's the best way to meet your reading purpose? If your purpose is to find out about the characters, conflict, and theme, the strategy of summarizing can help.

- **Use the strategy of summarizing to help you meet your purpose for reading the play.**

Directions: Record your notes on the Fiction Organizer on the next page. It can help you keep track of the most important elements of the play.

© GREAT SOURCE. ALL RIGHTS RESERVED.

NAME

FOR USE WITH PAGES 472–488

During Reading

Now go back and do a careful reading of *A Christmas Carol.* Make notes as you go.

D Read with a Purpose

Be sure to keep your reading purpose in mind as you read. Remember that you are searching for information about characters, conflict, and theme.

Directions: Interrupt your reading to make notes on this Fiction Organizer. It can help you meet your purpose.

Fiction Organizer

Characters

Setting

Title

Plot

© GREAT SOURCE. ALL RIGHTS RESERVED.

Using the Strategy

When you summarize, you tell the events of the plot in your own words. Sometimes you will want to summarize just one scene of a play—especially if the scene is an important one.

• Summarizing can help you process and remember what you've read.

Directions: Write your notes in the Magnet Summary below. Then summarize the scene you have just read from *A Christmas Carol*.

Magnet Summary

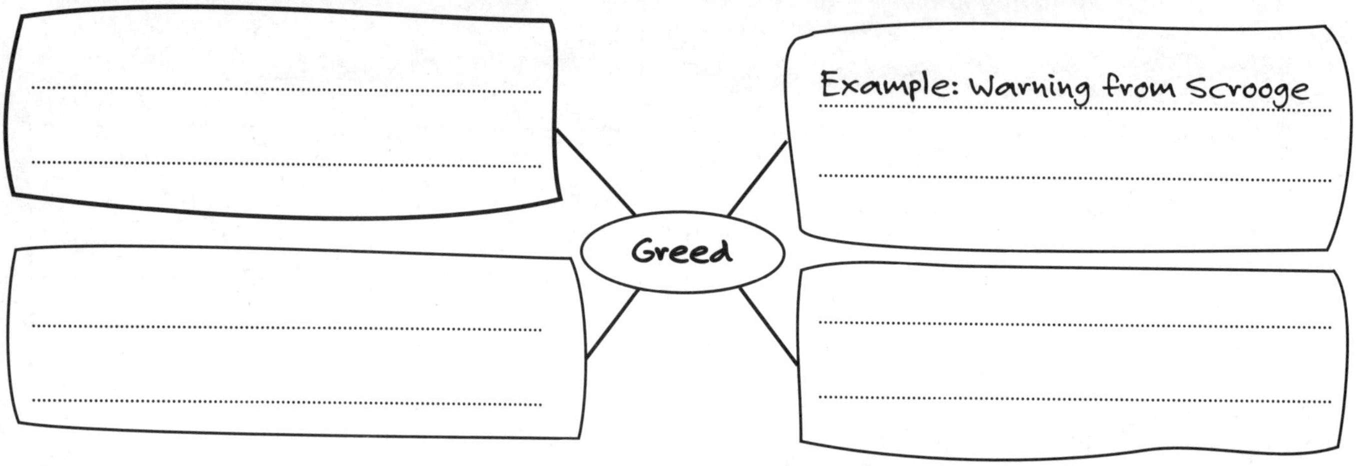

Summary

Understanding How Plays Are Organized

The plot of a play is organized around its conflict. The conflict is the main problem the characters must solve.

• To fully understand a play, you must examine the conflict.

Directions: Make notes about the conflict in this scene from *A Christmas Carol*. Then predict how you think things will turn out.

The conflict:

Here's how I predict the problem will be solved:

© GREAT SOURCE. ALL RIGHTS RESERVED.

NAME .... FOR USE WITH PAGES 472–488

E Connect

Making a personal connection to a play can help you understand its theme. One way of connecting is to tell your opinions of the characters.

- **Responding to the characters can help you uncover the theme of a play.**

Directions: Tell how you feel about Scrooge and Bob Cratchit. Then explain your opinion.

Here's how I feel about Scrooge: ....

....

I feel this way because ....

....

Here's how I feel about Bob Cratchit: ....

....

I feel this way because ....

....

After Reading

After you finish reading a play, take a moment to think about the theme. A theme is the playwright's message for the audience.

F Pause and Reflect

After reading, ask yourself about the characters, the conflict, and the theme.

- **After you finish a selection, go back to your original purpose and look for answers to your questions.**

Directions: How well did you meet your reading purpose? Make notes about any part of the scene that confuses or puzzles you.

....

....

© GREAT SOURCE. ALL RIGHTS RESERVED.

G Reread

At this point, you may want to think some more about the theme of the play. The rereading strategy of visualizing can help.

• Visualizing can help you "see" a play's theme.

Directions: Draw the scene in Scrooge's office.

H Remember

Good readers remember what they've read.

• To remember a play, memorize and then react to a key passage.

Directions: Choose a short passage from *A Christmas Carol* to memorize. Write the passage on the lines below. Then explain why you chose it.

Passage from A Christmas Carol:

Why I chose it:

© GREAT SOURCE. ALL RIGHTS RESERVED.

NAME .... FOR USE WITH PAGES 489-494

Focus on Theme

The theme of a play is the message or idea that the playwright wants you to remember. Most plays have a major theme and several minor themes. To find a play's themes, follow these steps.

Step 1: Find the "big ideas" or general topics.

Begin by asking yourself, "What is this play mostly about?"

Directions: Read this conversation between Bob Cratchit and his wife. Then get together with a small group. Decide how this dialogue supports what you already know about one of the topics in the play, greed.

from *A Christmas Carol*

(After their Christmas feast, the Cratchit family gathers around the hearth. BOB CRATCHIT *proposes a toast to Scrooge.)*

BOB CRATCHIT *(Cheerfully).* I'll give you Mr. Scrooge, the Founder of the Feast.

MRS. CRATCHIT *(Crying out).* The Founder of the Feast indeed. I wish I had him here. I'd give him a piece of my mind to feast upon.

BOB CRATCHIT. My dear, the children.

MRS. CRATCHIT. Why should we drink to the health of such a hateful, stingy, hard, and unfeeling man as Mr. Scrooge? You know he is, Bob. Nobody knows it better.

This dialogue shows ....

....

....

....

....

© GREAT SOURCE. ALL RIGHTS RESERVED.

Step 2: Find out what the characters do or say that relates to one of the general topics.

Directions: With a partner, choose two characters and discuss what they do and say about the topic of greed. Make notes here.

Double-entry Journal

Quote	My Notes
1.	
2.	

Step 3: Write a statement of the author's point or message about the general topic.

Be careful not to confuse a play's topic with its theme. The **topic** is what the play is about. The **theme** is the playwright's *message* about the topic.

Directions: Use this formula to find a theme in *A Christmas Carol*. Then write your reaction to the theme. Tell how the theme statement makes you feel. Do you agree or disagree with Dickens's message?

topic **+ what the author says about it** **= theme statement**

.... + ... = ...

I agree / disagree with his message because

© GREAT SOURCE. ALL RIGHTS RESERVED.

NAME

FOR USE WITH PAGES 495-501

Focus on Language

It's important to listen to a play's language. It can give you clues about character, plot, and theme.

Step 1: Think about key lines and speeches.

A character's speeches can help you understand his or her personality.

Directions: Read this speech from *A Christmas Carol*. Then write three adjectives (descriptive words) that describe Scrooge.

from *A Christmas Carol*

SCROOGE *(Angrily)*. You say Merry Christmas? Forget about Merry Christmas! What's Christmas time to you but a time for paying bills without money; a time for finding yourself a year older, but not an hour richer; a time for balancing your books and finding yourself deeply in debt? If I had my way, every person who wishes me a Merry Christmas would be boiled in his own pudding and buried with a stake through his heart!

This dialogue shows

Scrooge is , , and

Drama

Step 2: Read the stage directions.

Stage directions can help you "see" the events of a play.

Directions: Read these stage directions. Then sketch the scene's action on the Storyboard.

from *A Christmas Carol*

*(*SCROOGE *is in his office. He keeps his eye on his clerk,* BOB CRATCHIT, *who is copying letters. There is a small fire near* SCROOGE *and an even smaller one near* BOB CRATCHIT. *Suddenly, the door flies open and in steps Scrooge's nephew,* FRED.*)*

© GREAT SOURCE. ALL RIGHTS RESERVED.

Storyboard

1.	2.	3.

Step 3: Analyze the dialogue.

Dialogue can help you understand a play's theme. What does the conversation between Scrooge and Bob Cratchit say about greed?

from *A Christmas Carol*

SCROOGE. And yet you don't think me ill-used when I pay a day's wages for no work.

CRATCHIT. It's only once a year, sir.

SCROOGE *(Buttoning his coat to the chin)*. A poor excuse for picking a man's pocket every twenty-fifth of December. I suppose you must have the whole day. Be here all the earlier next morning.

Directions: Find a line in this conversation that supports a theme about greed. Write it in the Double-entry Journal. Then write your own thoughts about it.

Double-entry Journal

Quote	My Thoughts

© GREAT SOURCE. ALL RIGHTS RESERVED.

NAME .... FOR USE WITH PAGES 514–526

Reading a Website

Because most websites offer links from one spot on the Internet to another, it's easy to get lost. Also, not all websites give reliable information. A part of your job as critical reader is to carefully evaluate the information on a site and decide whether it can be trusted.

Before Reading

Practice using the reading process and strategy of reading critically to help you navigate a website that offers information about the common cold.

A Set a Purpose

Much of the time, you'll use the World Wide Web to find information about a specific subject.

- **To set your purpose, make a list of questions about the subject.**

Directions: Use this K-W-L Chart to record what you know about the common cold. Then write what you want to find out.

Internet

K-W-L Chart

What I Know	What I Want to Know	What I Learned
When I have a cold, my		
nose gets stuffed up.		
Use this section to tell what you already know about the common cold.	List your questions about the common cold here.	Save this section for later, after you've visited the website.

© GREAT SOURCE. ALL RIGHTS RESERVED.

B Preview

When you arrive at the website you're looking for, take a moment to survey it. Get a sense of what's offered before you begin clicking.

Directions: Preview the Common Cold website. Look for the items on this checklist. Make notes on what you find.

Preview Checklist

	My notes
Check the name and overall look of the site.	
Check the main menu or table of contents.	
Check the source or sponsor of the site.	
Check the first few lines describing the site.	
Check images or graphics that create a feeling for the site.	

© GREAT SOURCE. ALL RIGHTS RESERVED.

NAME FOR USE WITH PAGES 514-526

http://www.commoncold.cc.com*

En español

ABCs of Infectious Diseases

Center for Disease Control and Prevention

Facts

Complications

Cold Remedies

Preventives

Causes

Search

Chat

Email the ADA

The Common Cold Website

The common cold affects more humans in a given year than any other disease. Symptoms include cough, nasal congestion, runny nose, and sometimes fever. There is no known cure.

What will I find in the Common Cold website?

This site has been designed with the patient in mind. Link to the newest research and discoveries about the common cold. Use this website and other ADA websites for information on remedies, research, and prevention of various infectious diseases. Visit our chat room and compare notes with other patients.

The American Disease Association is a not-for-profit foundation dedicated to the study and treatment of the common cold and other infectious diseases. The ADA was founded nearly 70 years ago with the specific intent of researching infectious diseases in the U.S. and abroad. Dr. Elizabeth Cardlin, Ph.D., M.D., is director of this site. Direct your comments to her at www.cardlin@ada.com.

Students click here!

Last updated: July, 2002

For further information, contact:

The American Disease Association
2220 Beechwood Blvd.
Cleveland, OH 44106

About the ADA | News | Activities | Privacy Notice

* URL is not real.

Internet

© GREAT SOURCE. ALL RIGHTS RESERVED.

C Plan

Once you arrive at a website and decide on your purpose, you're ready to begin reading. Use the strategy of reading critically.

- **Reading critically means examining the information you're given and deciding whether or not it is reliable.**

Directions: Record your notes on the Website Profiler below to understand and evaluate elements of the website.

During Reading

Begin by examining the main menu, which runs along the left side of the site. Then let your eyes roam over the rest of the page.

D Read with a Purpose

As you skim the web page, focus on finding answers to your purpose questions. Make notes in the Website Profiler.

Website Profiler

Name	
URL	
Sponsor	Date
Point of View	Expertise
My Reaction	

© GREAT SOURCE. ALL RIGHTS RESERVED.

NAME .... FOR USE WITH PAGES 514–526

Using the Strategy

Reading critically means examining the website bit by bit. Remember that not every link will be useful to your purpose. Use Study Cards to keep track of important information at the site.

- **When you read critically, you decide which links will be useful to your purpose.**

Directions: Make some notes about the website on these cards. Which questions about the common cold that you wrote in the "What I Want to Know" column may be answered?

Keep your Study Cards in front of you as you link your way through the site.

Study Cards

What kinds of information does the site provide?

How does the information relate to my purpose?

Internet

© GREAT SOURCE. ALL RIGHTS RESERVED.

Understanding How Websites Are Organized

If you were to make a diagram of a website, you'd find that it really does look like a web. The "spokes" that reach out from the center of the web are paths that you may or may not want to follow.

Directions: Complete this Web about the common cold website. List four important links. Predict what you think you'll find there.

Web

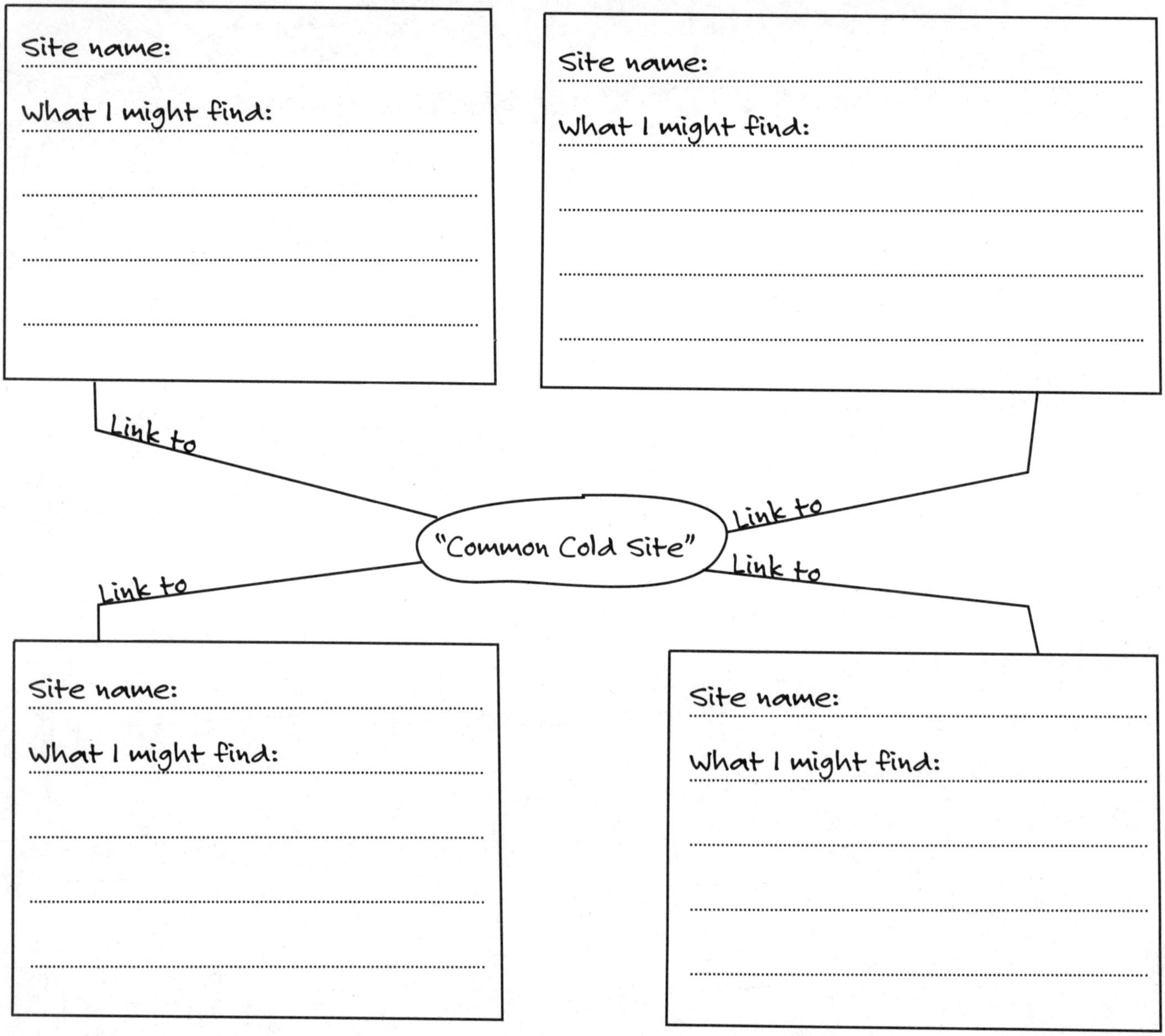

© GREAT SOURCE. ALL RIGHTS RESERVED.

NAME FOR USE WITH PAGES 514–526

E Connect

To "connect" with a website, take a moment to consider your own feelings about the topic or information.

• Decide whether or not the website is of use to you.

Directions: Think of three websites you've visited recently. Explain your opinion of each site and why you would or would not return.

Study Cards

Website #1

My opinion of it:

Why I would or would not return:

Website #2

My opinion of it:

Why I would or would not return:

Website #3

My opinion of it:

Why I would or would not return:

© GREAT SOURCE. ALL RIGHTS RESERVED.

After Reading

Take it slow and easy when researching on the Internet. Gather your thoughts before linking to the next site.

F Pause and Reflect

Recall your purpose for visiting the site. Return to the K-W-L Chart you created and make notes about what you learned.

- **After you visit a website, ask yourself, "How well did I meet my purpose?"**

Directions: Return to the K-W-L Chart on page 185. Make some notes in the "L" column. Then explain what else you'd like to learn.

I need to find out more about

G Reread

Sometimes you may need to look back at a site to double-check a fact or detail. At this point, you'll want to think carefully about whether or not the information on the site is reliable.

- **A powerful rereading strategy to use when checking for reliability is skimming.**

Directions: Complete this organizer. These are questions you should ask yourself when considering whether a site is reliable.

How to Evaluate Internet Sources

1. What is the source of the site?	2. What credentials does the site offer?	3. What is the purpose of the site?

© GREAT SOURCE. ALL RIGHTS RESERVED.

NAME

FOR USE WITH PAGES 514–526

How to Evaluate Internet Sources, continued

4. When was the site last updated?

5. Are there any obvious errors on the site, such as misspellings or typos?

H Remember

Good Internet researchers remember what they've read.

- **Summary Notes can help you remember a website.**

Directions: Write a list of the four main things you learned at the website. Refer to the notes you took during reading and the K-W-L Chart as needed.

Summary Notes

website: www.commoncold.cc.com

Four things I learned at the Common Cold website:

1.

2.

3.

4.

© GREAT SOURCE. ALL RIGHTS RESERVED.

Reading a Graphic

Much of the information you read at school and home will be in the form of a graphic. It's important that you know how to interpret graphics such as charts, graphs, maps, and diagrams. Practice reading and responding to them here.

Before Reading

The reading process works with graphics just as it does with text. Use the strategy of paraphrasing to help you get *more* from a graphic.

A Set a Purpose

Your purpose for reading a graphic is usually to answer two general questions: "What is the graphic about?" and "What does it say?"

• To set your purpose, ask two questions about the graphic.

Directions: Suppose you will be reading a graph about the sales of gas-guzzling vehicles between 1980 and 2005. Write two purpose-setting questions. Then make a prediction.

Purpose Question 1:

Purpose Question 2:

My prediction:

© GREAT SOURCE. ALL RIGHTS RESERVED.

NAME .... FOR USE WITH PAGES 538-547

B Preview the Reading

When you preview a graphic, look at the words as well as the illustration or picture.

• **The words and graphic itself are equally important.**

Directions: Preview the graphic below. Then make notes.

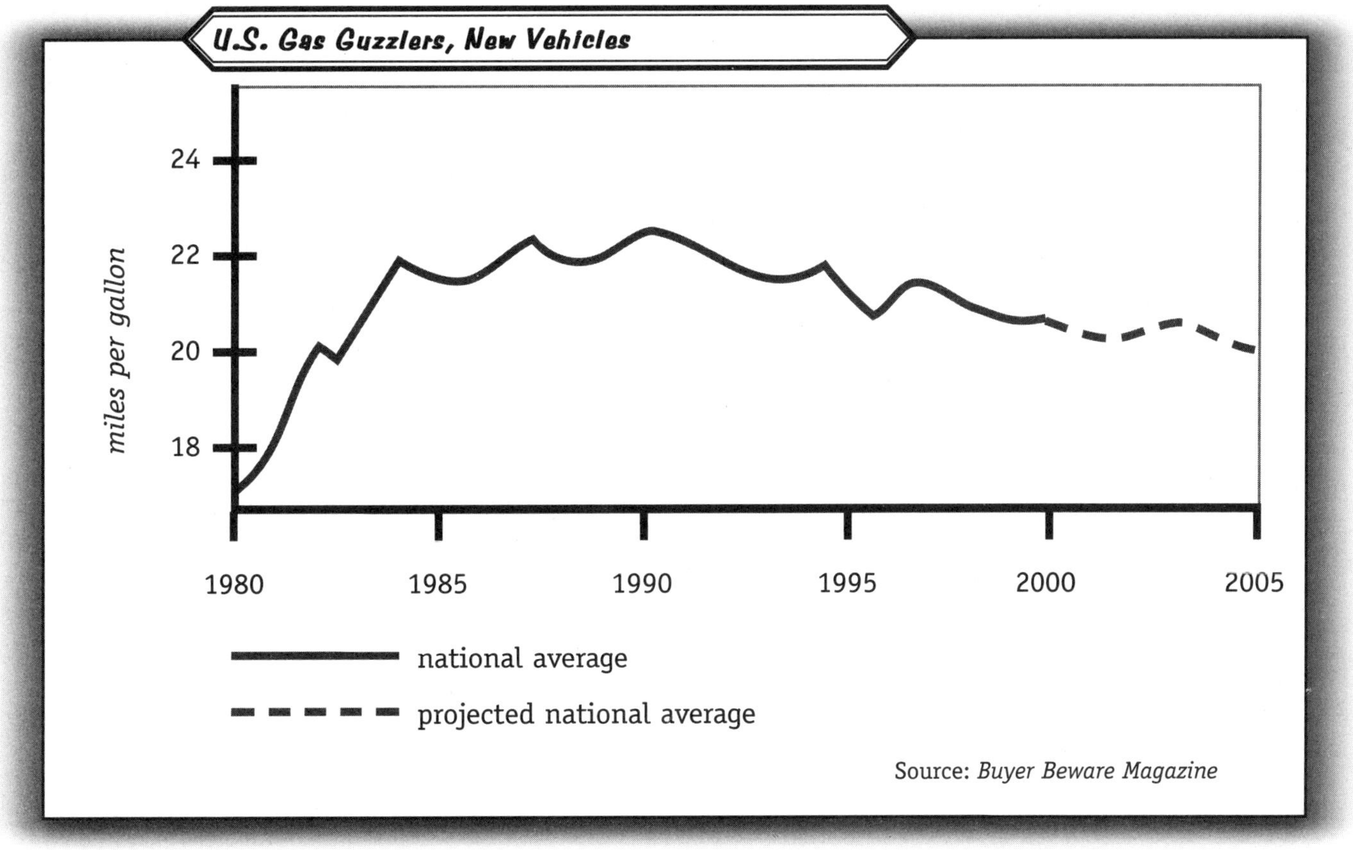

The title of the line graph is ....

The graph shows ....

....

The labels show ....

....

The source for the graphic is ....

....

© GREAT SOURCE. ALL RIGHTS RESERVED.

C Plan

Next make a plan. Choose a strategy that will help you read and interpret the graphic on page 195.

- **The strategy of paraphrasing can help you get *more* from a graphic.**

During Reading

Now turn your attention to the gas-guzzler line graph. First look at the graphic to gain an overall impression of what it shows. Then read the text.

D Read with a Purpose

Keep your purpose questions in mind as you read. Make notes about information that relates to these questions.

Directions: Read the gas-guzzler line graph. Then paraphrase, or tell in your own words, what the graphic shows.

The graphic shows this:

© GREAT SOURCE. ALL RIGHTS RESERVED.

NAME FOR USE WITH PAGES 538–547

Using the Strategy

Putting information from another source in your own words is called paraphrasing. Paraphrasing can help you process and remember information.

• Use a Paraphrase Chart to keep track of your ideas about the graphic.

Directions: Complete the Paraphrase Chart. It is started for you.

Paraphrase Chart

My Paraphrase

1. In 1990, vehicles got almost six more miles per gallon than in 1980.

2.

Graphics

Understanding How Graphics Are Organized

Understanding the parts of a graphic is key to unlocking what it says.

Directions: Label these elements on the graphic below: *title, legend, horizontal (x) axis,* and *vertical (y) axis*. If needed, review the definitions for these terms on pages 542–543 of your handbook.

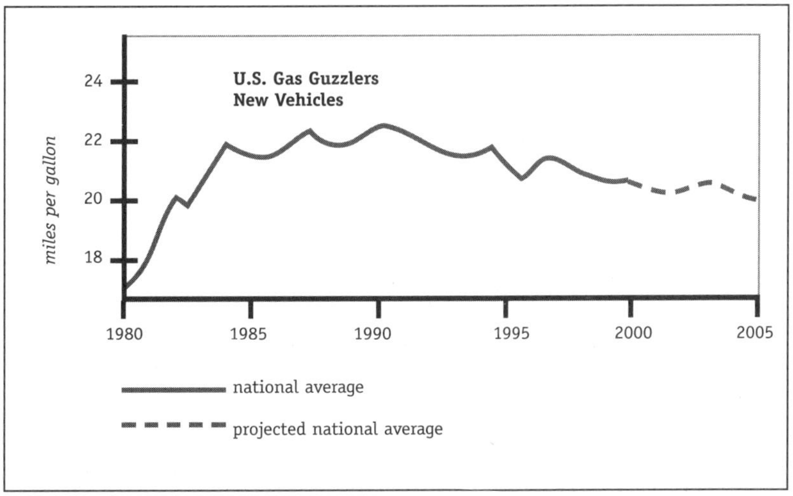

© GREAT SOURCE. ALL RIGHTS RESERVED.

E Connect

React to a graphic after you finish reading it.

• Add your thoughts and a personal connection to your Paraphrase Chart.

Paraphrase Chart

TITLE	GAS CONSUMPTION ISSUES
MY PARAPHRASE	
MY THOUGHTS	
CONNECTION	

After Reading

After you finish paraphrasing and reacting to a graphic, take a second to look at it to make sure you haven't missed anything.

F Pause and Reflect

First, think back to your reading purpose. Decide whether you've answered both questions.

• After you finish, ask yourself, "How well did I meet my purpose?"

Directions: Answer your purpose questions.

What is the graphic about?

What does it say?

© GREAT SOURCE. ALL RIGHTS RESERVED.

NAME

FOR USE WITH PAGES 538-547

G Reread

Look again at the graph about gas guzzlers. Ask yourself, "What conclusions can I draw?"

- **Use the rereading strategy of reading critically to help you draw some final conclusions about the graphic.**

Directions: Complete this chart. Refer to page 546 in your handbook if you get stuck.

Drawing Conclusions

Steps for Drawing Conclusions	My Notes
Is enough data presented to draw a good conclusion?	
Is the source reliable?	
Is there anything unusual about the way the data is presented? Is anything left out?	
What trends or other relationships do you see?	

H Remember

It's easy to remember a graphic if you actually *do* something with the information.

- **To remember a graphic, make a list.**

Directions: Make a list of facts and details you learned from reading the graphic about gas guzzlers.

Things I learned about gas-guzzling automobile sales:

© GREAT SOURCE. ALL RIGHTS RESERVED.

Reading a Test and Test Questions

Tests can't be avoided when you are a student. Here you'll learn ways that can help you prepare better and perform well on all kinds of tests.

Before Reading

You can prepare for a test by figuring out your purpose beforehand. Use the strategy of skimming to help you on tests.

A Set a Purpose

For any test, your purpose is twofold. Find out what the test questions are asking, and decide what information is needed for the answers.

• To set your purpose, ask a question about the test.

Directions: For this sample test, you'll read "Me and My Parents," an excerpt from an autobiography. Write your reading purpose here.

My purpose question:

B Preview

After you set your purpose, begin previewing. Try to get a sense of what is expected of you.

Directions: Skim the sample test that follows on the next two pages. Read the directions and take a quick look at the questions. Write what you notice on the sticky notes.

© GREAT SOURCE. ALL RIGHTS RESERVED.

NAME .... FOR USE WITH PAGES 564–579

I have this much time to complete the test:

....

....

English: Mid-year Reading Test

Mid-year Reading Test
30 Minutes — 5 Questions, 1 Essay

DIRECTIONS: Circle the letter of the correct answer. Write your essay in the blue test booklet.

You will not be penalized for incorrect answers.

I learned this from the directions:

....

....

....

....

MID-YEAR REVIEW, PASSAGE #1
"Me and My Parents"

In her autobiography, Haven "Zippy" Kimmel tells what it was like "growing up small in Mooreland, Indiana." Try to get a sense of what Kimmel was like as a child.

"Me and My Parents" from *A Girl Named Zippy* by Haven Kimmel

For one whole year I sighed every time I was asked to do anything. I felt incredibly put upon. My parents were patient with it for a few months, and then both began saying, in a rather clipped and hysterical way, *don't sigh,* immediately after making some request.

For instance, my dad might ask, "Have you done your feeding?" Which meant had I fed the few animals I had begged for and bet my life against, and I would stop what I was doing, which was probably sitting absolutely still watching *Gilligan's Island,* and sigh. And he would speedy-quick say *don't sigh,* but I was way ahead of him and had already done the sighing. Sometimes I would rouse myself and go feed the starving animals, but sometimes I would continue just very actively sitting there until he became agitated and got up to do it himself, meaning to shame me, which didn't work.

My parents went from reprimanding me to giving very thunderous looks, which also didn't stop me, until finally on one occasion, with the dogs howling for mercy outside, my father snapped. I was standing in the doorway between the living room and the den, and he covered the distance so quickly he appeared to levitate. He took me by the shoulders and backed me all the way down the length of the long living room, his face in mine, staring at me like a deranged cow, saying over and over, *don't sigh,* through his clenched teeth. So I stopped sighing.

I predict the reading will be about this:

....

....

....

....

Tests

© GREAT SOURCE. ALL RIGHTS RESERVED.

PASSAGE #1 MULTIPLE-CHOICE QUESTIONS

I noticed this about the test questions:

1. The author of this passage is ____.

A. Mr. Kimmel
B. Mrs. Kimmel
C. Zippy Kimmel
D. a childhood friend of Zippy's

2. Zippy sighs because _____.

A. she feels put upon
B. she likes to tease her parents
C. she is tired
D. she is bored

3. The tone of the passage is _____.

A. sad
B. suspenseful
C. solemn
D. humorous

4. How do Zippy's parents react when she first starts sighing?

A. They are patient for a while.
B. They are annoyed right from the beginning.
C. They take her aside and explain why it bothers them.
D. They threaten to take away the TV.

5. What finally causes Zippy's father to "snap"?

A. *Gilligan's Island*
B. a new dog
C. Zippy's lack of shame
D. his wife's hysteria

PASSAGE #1 ESSAY QUESTION

Write a description of Zippy. To get started, think of two adjectives (descriptive words) you can use in your essay. Support your description with evidence. Then check your essay for errors.

© GREAT SOURCE. ALL RIGHTS RESERVED.

NAME

FOR USE WITH PAGES 564-579

C Plan

Most of the tests you take in school will have a combination of factual recall and critical thinking questions. What you need is a strategy that can help you answer both types of questions.

- **Use the strategy of skimming to help you find answers.**

During Reading

At first read the passage slowly and carefully. It's a mistake to rush through to get to the questions.

D Read with a Purpose

As you read, think about your purpose. Use a highlighter to mark important sentences. Look for the author's main point.

Directions: Read "Me and My Parents." Highlight the most important sentences. Then tell what you think the author's main idea is.

I think Kimmel's main idea is this:

Using the Strategy

After you read the article, problem, or test item, take a look at the test questions. Read each one carefully. Then skim the reading for answers.

- **Skim the passage for answers to the questions. Look for details that might relate to the author's main point.**

Directions: Read the multiple-choice test questions. Then tell where you will skim to find the answers.

Question #	Where I'll begin skimming
1	I remember something about this in the introduction. So I'll start there.
2	
3	
4	
5	

Tests

© GREAT SOURCE. ALL RIGHTS RESERVED.

Understanding How Tests Are Organized

Many tests end with one or more essay questions.

Directions: Read the essay question carefully. Make notes.

English: Mid-year Reading Test

Write a description of Zippy. To get started, think of two adjectives (descriptive words) you can use in your essay. Support your description with evidence. Then check your essay for errors.

1. What type of essay will you write?

2. What is the topic?

3. What will your thesis statement be?

Zippy is

and

4. What details will you use to support your thesis?

E Connect

When you can, make personal connections to tests. Write your comments in the margin of the booklet. Use these comments to help you answer the open-ended questions.

- **Record your reactions to the person, place, or thing described in a test passage.**

Directions: Write your opinion of Zippy. Then add three details that describe Zippy. Try to think of words not used in the passage.

Opinion Statement

Here's what I think about Zippy:

Supporting Details:

© GREAT SOURCE. ALL RIGHTS RESERVED.

NAME

FOR USE WITH PAGES 564-579

After Reading

Once you've completed the test, take a moment to gather your thoughts.

F Pause and Reflect

First, check to be sure that you've answered every question. Then ask yourself, "Have I answered each question to the best of my ability?"

- **After you finish a test, return to the questions that gave you the most difficulty and double-check your answers.**

Directions: How well did you do on the test? Make notes about which question was difficult and the strategy of skimming.

This is the multiple-choice question that I found most difficult:

Here's why:

Here's how the strategy of skimming helped me answer the question:

Tests

© GREAT SOURCE. ALL RIGHTS RESERVED.

G Reread

When you finish the easiest questions on the test, return to the challenging ones. These are often inference or conclusion questions.

- **Read at least three sentences to answer each question.**

Directions: Read this inference question. Then write a Think Aloud that tells how you will figure out the answer.

7. Why does Zippy stop sighing?

A. She feels guilty about the dogs.
B. Her father's anger frightens her.
C. She develops a sore throat.
D. Her mother and father beg her to.

Think Aloud

To help me answer this question

© GREAT SOURCE. ALL RIGHTS RESERVED.

NAME .... FOR USE WITH PAGES 564–579

H Remember

Take a careful look at a test after your teacher has graded it. Figure out what you did wrong so that you can avoid making the same mistakes in the future.

- **Remember the test questions that gave you the most trouble. Similar questions may appear on future tests.**

Directions: Exchange tests with a classmate. "Grade" each other's tests, and comment on them. Then write what *you* can do to improve your test-taking abilities.

I can improve my test-taking abilities by

© GREAT SOURCE. ALL RIGHTS RESERVED.

Focus on Essay Tests

Essay tests are not as hard as you think. What you need is a plan that you can follow from the beginning of the test to the end.

Step 1: Read carefully.

Take time to read the directions and writing prompt very carefully. Mark key words and phrases. Think about the type of essay you are asked to write. What is the topic? What must be in your essay? What do you do when you're done?

Directions: Read this essay assignment and prompt. Underline key words and phrases. Then retell the assignment on the sticky note.

The 5 things I need to do as I write this essay:

1. ....

2. ....

3. ....

4. ....

5. ....

DIRECTIONS: Write an opinion essay about a new rule at your local mall. First read the prompt below. Then write your opinion statement. Next offer support for your opinion. Carefully proofread your writing when you're done.

Prompt: Your local mall has a new rule that anyone under sixteen must be accompanied by an adult at all times while on mall property. How do you feel about this rule? Write an essay stating your opinion. Support it with convincing evidence.

© GREAT SOURCE. ALL RIGHTS RESERVED.

NAME FOR USE WITH PAGES 580-583

Step 2: Plan your essay.

It's extremely important that you take the time to organize your essay before you begin writing.

Directions: Use this Main Idea Organizer to plan your essay.

Main Idea Organizer

Your Opinion:		
Supporting Detail 1	Supporting Detail 2	Supporting Detail 3
Concluding Sentence:		

Step 3: Write.

Refer to your organizer as you write. In your introduction, state your opinion. In the body of the essay, give evidence that supports the opinion. In the conclusion, restate your opinion.

Directions: Write the first sentence or introductory paragraph for your essay here.

Step 4: Proofread.

Remember that errors can affect your score. Check for problems in spelling, punctuation, and usage.

Directions: Proofread and correct the paragraph you just wrote.

© GREAT SOURCE. ALL RIGHTS RESERVED.

Focus on Vocabulary Tests

To do well on a vocabulary test, you must have a good knowledge of words and word parts. You also must be able to understand the relationship between words in an analogy. Follow these steps.

Step 1: Preview.

Begin by skimming the test questions. Are the questions fill-in-the-blank or multiple-choice? Then highlight vocabulary terms such as *synonym, antonym,* and *analogy.*

Directions: Preview this Sample Test. Highlight an important vocabulary term.

Sample Test

DIRECTIONS: Find the synonym for each underlined word.

1. The day was so hot and I was so parched that I ran for the hose.
   A. tired B. hot C. thirsty D. winded

2. We pinched our noses when we smelled the skunk's repulsive odor.
   A. disgusting B. fragrant C. unusual D. fresh

3. Mom is hooked on that engrossing new television drama and won't miss it for anything.
   A. gripping B. boring C. routine D. unexciting

Step 2: Eliminate wrong answers.

First eliminate answers that are clearly wrong.

Directions: Look at the questions again. Cross out the answers you know are *wrong.*

© GREAT SOURCE. ALL RIGHTS RESERVED.

NAME FOR USE WITH PAGES 584-587

Step 3: Use context clues.

Next, check the words near the unknown word. Look for clues about the unknown word's meaning.

Directions: Reread question #1. What context clues do you find for the word *parched?*

Context Clue #1: What it tells me:

Context Clue #2: What it tells me:

Step 4: Figure out word relationships.

To solve an analogy, first figure out how the word pair is related. Then choose another pair that has the same relationship.

Directions: First, review the section on word analogies in your handbook (pages 636–639). Then tell the relationship between the words *flower* and *tulip*. Finish by solving the analogy.

Sample Test

1. flower : tulip ::
   A. tree : pests
   B. grass : forest
   C. picnic : basket
   D. animal : cat

These two words are related because

.

The correct answer is because .

Step 5: Check.

Save four or five minutes at the end of the test so that you can check your work.

Directions: Answer the questions on the Sample Test. Then compare answers with a classmate's answers. If you disagree, explain your thinking.

Tests

© GREAT SOURCE. ALL RIGHTS RESERVED.

Focus on Social Studies Tests

Social studies tests usually focus on names and places, dates and events, and big ideas in history. Follow these steps to improve your score.

Step 1: Preview.

Quickly skim the test. Get a feeling for the kinds of questions on it. Mark the "easy" questions you'll want to answer first.

Directions: Take a quick look at the Sample Test. Highlight the most important words.

Sample Test

1. Beginning in 1810, General Simón Bolivar led Venezuela in a fight for independence from what country?
   A. Peru
   B. Spain
   C. the United States
   D. Central America

2. What name was given to the new republic organized in southern Peru around 1830 to honor the man who led Venezuela to independence?
   A. Bolivia
   B. Peru
   C. Colombia
   D. New Spain

3. Which of the following was the most significant influence on the culture of Venezuela?
   A. Immigrants from Europe
   B. The North Americans
   C. Immigrants from China
   D. The Spanish conquerors

Step 2: Rule out wrong answers.

If you don't know the right answer immediately, look for answers you know are *wrong*.

Directions: Return to the sample questions. Cross out the answers you know are wrong. (Hints: For question #1, remember that you are looking for the name of a *country*. For question #2, what name might come from the name of an important leader? For question #3, what do you know about the culture of South America?)

© GREAT SOURCE. ALL RIGHTS RESERVED.

NAME .... FOR USE WITH PAGES 588-592

Step 3: Reread the question.

Reread the question until you're sure you know what it's asking.

Directions: Complete the sentence started below.

Question #1 wants me to figure out ....

....

Step 4: Talk your way through the possible answers.

Think through the remaining answers to the question.

Directions: Complete this Think Aloud for question #1.

Think Aloud

I know that answer D is wrong because Central America is not a country.

I also think .... might be wrong because ....

....

Step 5: Choose an answer and double-check.

Finally, make your choice. Then reread the question one more time to see if the answer you've chosen makes sense.

Directions: Write what you think is the correct answer to question #1. Then explain your choice.

My answer: .... **My explanation:** ....

....

....

....

....

Tests

© GREAT SOURCE. ALL RIGHTS RESERVED.

Focus on Math Tests

Math tests require your undivided attention from start to finish. Remember that the questions probably will become progressively more difficult as you go. Follow these steps to improve your score.

Step 1: Preview.

Always begin with a preview. Look for the most important information in each question.

Directions: Preview this Sample Test. Highlight the most important parts.

Sample Test

1. Tre scored 93, 95, 70, 78, and 89 on this year's math quizzes. He scored 90, 93, 87, 90, and 70 on this year's science quizzes. What is his average score in each class?
   A. Math 77 Science 79 C. Math 85 Science 86
   B. Math 93 Science 97 D. Math 87 Science 83

2. Kim scored 65, 90, 86, and 95 on this year's essay tests. She scored 95, 75, 72, and 78 on last year's essay tests. What is her average score for each year?
   A. This year 90 Last year 85 C. This year 70 Last year 75
   B. This year 84 Last year 80 D. This year 80 Last year 84

Step 2: Eliminate wrong answers.

Whenever possible, use number sense to eliminate answers that are clearly *wrong*.

Directions: Return to the sample questions. Cross out the answers that are clearly wrong. (Hint: A set of scores might be too high or too low.)

© GREAT SOURCE. ALL RIGHTS RESERVED.

NAME ________________ FOR USE WITH PAGES 593-597

Step 3: Estimate.

Always estimate the answer if you can. Doing some rough calculations may help you rule out another answer or two.

Directions: Look at question #1 again. Then decide. Should Tre's math or science average be higher?

I estimate that his ________________ average should be higher.

Step 4: Visualize.

Try to visualize what the problem is asking. Visualizing can make the problem easier to understand.

Directions: Make a sketch for what question #1 is asking.

Step 5: Check.

Whenever possible, check your work by using a different method to solve the same problem.

Directions: Rewrite question #1 as an equation. Write one equation to figure out the math score and one to figure out the science score.

Math equation: ________________

Science equation: ________________

© GREAT SOURCE. ALL RIGHTS RESERVED.

Focus on Science Tests

To succeed on a science test, you must think like a scientist and use the scientific method. Follow these steps.

Step 1: Prepare for the test.

Make visuals to help you remember information. Review your notes. Skim for key words and their definitions. Look again at the graphics.

Directions: Read the chart and then make notes about which animals live on land, which live in water, and which spend most of their time in the air.

Animal Facts

Characteristics	Animal	Information
fastest on land	cheetah	70 m.p.h.
fastest through air	swift	105 m.p.h.
deepest diver	sperm whale	6,000–7,000 ft.
largest water animal	blue whale	150 tons
largest land animal	African elephant	5 tons
smallest primate	mouse lemur	.1–.2 lb.

Land	Water	Air

© GREAT SOURCE. ALL RIGHTS RESERVED.

NAME FOR USE WITH PAGES 598–605

Step 2: Preview the test.

When the test is distributed, read the questions quickly to see what you will need to answer. Mark the easier questions. Glance at any graphics.

Directions: Do a Think Aloud to explain how you would use the chart in Step 1 to answer the following test questions.

Sample Test

DIRECTIONS: Use the chart "Animal Facts." Write the answers.

1. What is the largest land mammal on earth?

2. Which land animals on the chart are **slower** than the cheetah?

Think Aloud

Question 1 asks me to ________ so I'll look at the chart and ________.

Question 2 asks me to ________ so I'll look at the chart and ________.

Step 3: Check.

Save a few minutes of the test period to check your work. Scan for careless mistakes, and reread questions and your answers as time permits.

Directions: Check your work by rewriting the questions and answers as statements. Then check to see if the statements are true.

Question #1 rewritten as a statement:

Question #2 rewritten as a statement:

© GREAT SOURCE. ALL RIGHTS RESERVED.

Learning New Words

Words are something you'll want to collect. You don't want just one or two—you want lots and lots of them. Follow these steps to build your vocabulary.

Step 1: Read.

When you come to an unfamiliar word in your reading, take the time to "collect" it.

Directions: Read this passage. Circle words that are unfamiliar to you.

from "Little Selves" by Mary Lerner

Margaret O'Brien, a great-aunt and seventy-five, knew she was near the end. She did not repine, for she had had a long, hard life and she was tired. The young priest who brought her communion had administered the last rites—holy oils on her eyelids (Lord, forgive her the sins of seeing!); holy oils on her lips (Lord, forgive her the sins of speaking!), on her ears, on her knotted hands, on her weary feet. Now she was ready, though she knew the approach of the dread presence would mean greater suffering. So she folded quiet her hands beneath her heart, there where no child had ever lain, yet where now something grew and fattened on her strength. And she seemed given over to pleasant reverie.

Step 2: Record.

Keep a running list of unfamiliar words in your reading journal. Remember to write where you first noticed a word.

© GREAT SOURCE. ALL RIGHTS RESERVED.

NAME FOR USE WITH PAGES 608–614

Directions: Write the words you circled in the story.

Vocabulary Journal

English

from "Little Selves,"

Unfamiliar Words	Definitions

Step 3: Define.

Use a dictionary to figure out the meaning of each word on your list.

Directions: Get together with a partner. Choose the dictionary definition that relates to the way the word is used in the story. Write the definitions on the journal page above.

Step 4: Use new words.

The best way to remember a new word is to use it in conversation or in writing.

Directions: With your partner, write sentences for the words on your journal page.

© GREAT SOURCE. ALL RIGHTS RESERVED.

Building Vocabulary

To build your vocabulary, learn how to use context and some basic word parts. You can practice here.

Step 1: Use context clues.

Use context clues to figure out the meaning of unknown words.

Directions: Read this excerpt from Judith Ortiz Cofer's autobiography. Try using context clues to figure out the meaning of the underlined words.

from *Silent Dancing* by Judith Ortiz Cofer

In Mamá's house (everyone called my grandmother Mamá) was a large parlor built by my grandfather to his wife's exact specifications so that it was always cool, facing away from the sun. The doorway was on the side of the house so no one could walk directly into her living room. First they had to take a little stroll through and around her beautiful garden where prize-winning orchids grew in the trunk of an ancient tree she hollowed out for that purpose.

Underlined Words	My Definition	Context Clues I Used
parlor	living room	Near where **parlor** appears, I see the word **living room.** I think **parlor** is another word for **living room.**
specifications		
stroll		
hollowed		

© GREAT SOURCE. ALL RIGHTS RESERVED.

NAME ____________________ FOR USE WITH PAGES 615–625

Step 2: Use word parts.

Word parts are roots, prefixes, and suffixes. Knowing various word parts can quickly multiply the number of new words you can understand. Practice using roots, prefixes, and suffixes here.

Directions: Complete this Web.

Add words that have the root *photo.*

Roots

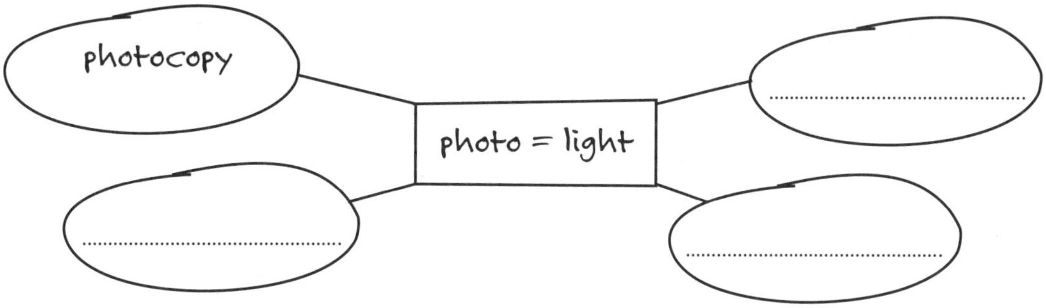

Prefixes

dis- = not, opposite   *over-* = too much   *re-* = again

Directions: Add a prefix from the box to the beginning of each word. The result is a whole new word. Then tell what the word means.

Prefix	+ Word	= New Word	Meaning of New Word
	+ appear	=	
	+ write	=	
	+ due	=	

Suffixes

-en = to make   *-less* = without

Directions: Remember that a suffix changes the way the word is used in a sentence. Write a sentence for each word. Underline the word.

fright + -en   Sentence: ____________________

____

thought + -less   Sentence: ____________________

____

Vocabulary

© GREAT SOURCE. ALL RIGHTS RESERVED.

Dictionary Dipping

Knowing what's in a dictionary can help you find words quickly and efficiently. Practice reading a dictionary entry here.

Step 1: Read.

Once you've found the entry for a word, read it carefully. Make notes to help you remember.

Directions: Answer the questions about this entry for *chasm*. Review page 629 in your handbook if you get stuck.

> **chasm** (kaz′ əm) *n.* 1. A deep opening or crack in the earth; gap. 2. A large difference in feelings or interests between people or groups. [from the Latin *chasma.*] *plural* **chasms.**

How many definitions does *chasm* have? ....

What is the history of the word? ....

What part of speech is *chasm?* ....

What is the plural of *chasm?* ....

Step 2: Remember.

A good way to remember a new word is to use it.

Directions: Write two sentences with the word *chasm*.

Sentence #1: ....

....

Sentence #2: ....

....

© GREAT SOURCE. ALL RIGHTS RESERVED.

NAME .... FOR USE WITH PAGE 630

Reading a Thesaurus

A thesaurus can open your eyes to dozens of new words. Practice reading a thesaurus entry here.

Step 1: Read the entry.

Once you've found the word you're looking for, read all its synonyms. Make a note of the ones you think would work best.

Directions: Read the entry for *embarrassing*. Then answer these questions. Review page 630 in your handbook if you get stuck.

Thesaurus Entry

embarrassing *adjective* difficult, disturbing, confusing, bewildering, puzzling, rattling, perplexing, delicate, distressing, humiliating, upsetting, awkward, troublesome, worrisome, uncomfortable, inconvenient, helpless.—**Antonyms:** [*adjective*] comfortable, easy, agreeable.

What part of speech is *embarrassing?* ....

What are some synonyms for *embarrassing?* ....

What are some antonyms? ....

Step 2: Use the synonyms.

Practice using the synonyms you found.

Directions: Complete this paragraph using synonyms for *embarrassing*.

My parents gave me a surprise party. It was so embarrassing! When I walked into the room, everyone yelled, "Surprise!" and it was really .... My parents gave me a big hug, and that made everything even more ....

© GREAT SOURCE. ALL RIGHTS RESERVED.

Vocabulary

Author/Title Index

Photo Credits

22 ©Erich Lessing/Art Resource, NY

32 ©Hulton/Archive by Getty Images

41 ©Corbis

42 ©Photodisc

81 courtesy Library of Congress

101 ©Corbis

© GREAT SOURCE. ALL RIGHTS RESERVED.